PACIFIC RIM
DISCOVERY
STUDENT RESOURCE

Michael W. Cranny, M.A.
Humanities Department Head
Fraser Lake Secondary School
BRITISH COLUMBIA

Stan Garrod, M.A.
Head of Social Studies
Collingwood School
BRITISH COLUMBIA

Margit McGuire, PH.D.
Professor and Chair of Teacher Education
at Seattle University
WASHINGTON

Contributing Writer:
Gary Birchall, B.A.
Barton Secondary School
HAMILTON, ONTARIO

Cartography by
Mapping Specialists Limited
MADISON, WISCONSIN

Nelson Canada
I(T)P An International Thomson Publishing Company

Toronto • Albany • Bonn • Boston • Cincinnati • Detroit • London • Madrid • Melbourne
Mexico City • New York • Pacific Grove • Paris • San Francisco • Singapore • Tokyo • Washington

I(T)P™
International Thomson Publishing
The trademark ITP is used under license

Published in 1995 by
Nelson Canada,
A Division of Thomson Canada Limited
1120 Birchmount Road
Scarborough, Ontario M1K 5G4

Canadian Cataloguing in Publication Data

Cranny, Michael William, 1947–
Pacific Rim discovery : student resource

Includes index.
ISBN 0–17–604681–X

1. East Asia – Social life and customs – Juvenile literature. 2. East Asia – History – Juvenile literature. 3. East Asia – Geography – Juvenile literature. I. Garrod, Stan. II. McGuire, Margit. III. Title.

DS504.5.C7 1994 950 C94–931441–2

Executive Editors: Joseph Gladstone, Jean Stinson
Project Coordinator: Jeffrey Aberle
Developmental Editors: Muriel Napier, Linda Scott, Jeffrey Aberle
Cartographic Consultant: Karen Ewing
Data Research: Ann Ludbrook
Photo Research: Elizabeth Fowler, Natalie Pavlenko Lomaga, Ann Ludbrook
Senior Production Editor: Deborah Lonergan
Graphic Communications Manager: Deborah Woodman
Art Director: Liz Nyman
Design and Composition: First Image
Illustrations: Henry Van Der Linde, Eric Colquhoun, Sarah Jane English
Graphs: First Image
Cover Images: beach: G. Motil/First Light;
panda: ©Frans Lanting, Minden Pictures/First Light;
train:©Dallas & John Heaton/First Light;
man with camels: Eric Colquhoun

Reviewers
The publishers thank the following people who contributed their valuable expertise during the development of this book:

Dr. John Alwin *Associate Professor of Geography*
Central Washington University, Ellensburg

Wayne Axford
Burnaby School Board

Tony Burley *Coordinator of Instruction*
Red Deer Public School Board

Jim Campbell *Supervisor, Social Studies*
Calgary Board of Education

R. James Crewe *Program Coordinator (Social Studies)*
Pentecostal Assemblies Board of Education, Grand Falls-Windsor

Charles Kahn *Writer/Editor*
Salt Spring Island, B.C.

Bill Larkin *Co-ordinator, Senior and Global Education*
East York Board of Education

John Lohrenz *Consultant, Social Studies*
Manitoba Education and Training

Geoffrey J. Matthews *Chief Cartographer*
University of Toronto

Roger Middleton
Durham Board of Education

Judy Morrison *Program Consultant*
Burnaby School Board

Ken Noma
East York Board of Education

Neil Taylor
School District #1, Winnipeg

Brenda Wallace
Faculty of Education, University of Calgary

Printed and bound in Canada
1 2 3 4 5 6 7 8 9 0 / B P / 3 2 1 0 9 8 7 6 5 4

Photo Credits

l: left **c:** center **r:** right **t:** top **m:** middle **b:** bottom

p. 10: National Archives of Canada; **p. 11:** Schuster/Scholz–Publiphoto; **p. 14:** Canapress Photo Service; **p. 15:** l & t r: U.S. Geological Survey, b r: J. D. Griggs/U.S. Geological Survey; **p. 16:** Wiley Photo Files; **p. 17:** P. Baeza/Publiphoto; **p. 19:** l: The Houston Post, r: Patrick Riviere/Ponopresse; **p. 20:** t: V. Last/Geographical Visual Aids, b l: Myra Ottewell, b r: CIDA Photo/Dilip Mehta; **p. 21:** t l: D. Aubert/Sygma–Publiphoto, t r: Kees/Sygma–Publiphoto, b l: Wiley Photo Files, b r: Reuters/Bettman; **p. 22:** t l & t r & b l: Wiley Photo Files, b r: R. Grace/Greenpeace; **p. 23:** t & b: Wiley Photo Files, m: Dept. Of Fisheries and Oceans, Sydney, B. C.; **p. 24:** l: Robin White/Fotolex Associates, r: A. Penner; **p. 25:** t l: Y. Y. Shopov, McMaster University, t r: Brian Milne/First Light, m l: Wiley Photo Files, m r: A. Penner, b: V. Last/Geographical Visual Aids; **p. 26:** CIDA Photo/Frank Koller; **p. 27:** t: Wiley Photo Files, b: CIDA Photo/Virginia Boyd; **p. 28:** l: Wiley Photo Files, r: Japan Information Centre, Consulate General of Japan; **p. 29:** l: Charles Philip/First Light, r: Japan Information Centre, Consulate General Of Japan; **p. 30:** l: R. Perry/Sygma–Publiphoto, r: CIDA Photo/Roger Lemoyne; **p. 31:** t: J. Bernier/Publiphoto, m l: Sygma–Publiphoto, m c: CIDA Photo/David Barbour, m r: J. Bryson/Sygma–Publiphoto, b: Y. Beaulieu/Publiphoto; **p. 32:** CIDA Photo/David Barbour; **p. 33:** t: CIDA Photo/David Barbour, b: Sunnybrook Health Science Centre; **p. 34:** t: P. McCowan/Geographical Visual Aids, m: Pierre Toutian Dorbec/Sygma–Publiphoto, b: V. Last/Geographical Visual Aids; **p. 35:** New Zealand Tourism Board; **p. 36:** l: Robin White/Fotolex Associates, c: V. Last/Geographical Visual Aids, r: Wiley Photo Files; **p. 37:** Wiley Photo Files; **p. 39:** l & r: Royal Ontario Museum; **p. 42:** t: Stan Garrod, b: Myra Ottewell; **p. 43:** t l: Singapore Tourist Promotion Board, t c: P. McCowan/Geographical Visual Aids, t r: Japan National Tourist Organization, b l: N. S. Ranadive, b l c: Government of India Tourist Office, b c r & b r: Stan Garrod; **p. 45:** t r & m r & m c & b r: Government of India Tourist Office, m l: A. E. Sirulnikoff/First Light, b l: Patrick Glaize/Publiphoto; **p. 46:** l: N. S. Ranadive, r: Government of India Tourist Office; **p. 47:** t l: Government of India Tourist Office, b l: Sygma–Publiphoto, r: Keystone/Sygma–Publiphoto; **p. 48:** t & b: Myra Ottewell; **p. 50:** l: Christine Spencer/Sygma–Publiphoto; t r & b r: J. Langevin/Sygma–Publiphoto; **p. 51:** t l & m l & r: Wiley Photo Files, b l: Stan Garrod; **p. 52:** t l: Camilla Jenkins, t r: Wesley Anderson, b r: A. Penner, b l: B. Basin/Publiphoto; **p. 53:** l: Earth Satellite Corporation, t r: Camilla Jenkins, b r: Comstock Photography; **p. 54:** b l: L. Zylberman/Sygma–Publiphoto, t c: Imapress/P. H. Bernard Martinez/Ponopresse, t r: Patrick Aventurier/Ponopresse; **p. 55:** all photos: Singapore Tourist Promotion Board; **p. 56:** b l: Birgitte Nielson, b c & b r: Wiley Photo Files; **p. 57:** l: Stan Garrod, r: Hong Kong Government Photo; **p. 59:** t r: Wiley Photo Files, m l & m r & b l & b r: Andrew Marton, b c: Valdin/Diaf/Publiphoto; **p. 60:** t l: Wiley Photo Files, t r & b l & b r: Andrew Marton; **p. 61:** all photos: Andrew Marton; **p. 62:** t: Xin-Hua/Sygma–Publiphoto, b: Comstock Photography; **p. 63:** l: J. Lauzon/Publiphoto, c: Schuster–Publiphoto, r: J. Loiseau/Diaf/Publiphoto; **p. 64:** Birgitte Nielson; **p. 65:** l & r: Korean Overseas Information Centre; **p. 66:** t: Japan Information Centre, Consulate General of Japan, b l: Stan Garrod, b r: Japan National Tourist Organization; **p. 67:** t l & t r & b r: Japan Information Centre, Consulate General of Japan, b l: Wiley Photo Files; **p. 68:** r m & c: Japan Information Centre, Consulate General of Japan, t r & b r: Stan Garrod, b l: The Granger Collection; **p. 69:** t: Stan Garrod, m l & b r: Japan Information Centre, Consulate General of Japan, b l: The Granger Collection; **p. 71:** t l & t r & m r b & b r & b l: Japan Information Centre, Consulate General of Japan, m r t & m l & b m: Japan National Tourist Organization; **p. 72:** Sovphoto; **p. 73:** all photos: Sovphoto; **p. 74:** both photos: Wiley Photo Files; **p. 75:** t: Bob Mansour, b: Comstock Photography; **p. 76:** t l & b l: Wiley Photo Files, m l t: A. Penner, m l b: British Columbia Tourism, b r: Wiley Photo Files; **p. 77:** both photos: Wiley Photo Files, b l: detail of "Captain Cook meets the West Coast Indians at Nootka, 1778", National Archives of Canada, Negative C-73721; **p. 78:** t: A. Penner, b: Wiley Photo Files; **p. 79:** t r: Ira Block/Image Bank, b l: A. Penner, b r: Wiley Photo Files; **p. 80:** D. Muench/Comstock Photography; **p. 81:** both photos: Wiley Photo Files; **p. 82:** t l: Jean Marie Jro/Valan Photos, t r: Robin White/Fotolex Associates, b l: Anthony Scullion/Valan Photos, b r: Paul G. Adam/Publiphoto; **p. 84:** l: I. Campion/Sygma–Publiphoto, t r & b r: V. Last/Geographical Visual Aids; **p. 85:** t: Kevin Brice/Sygma–Publiphoto, b: Comstock Photography; **p. 86:** Australian Tourist Commission; **p. 87:** l: Wiley Photo Files, t r & b r: New Zealand Tourism Board; **p. 89:** t r: Jacaranda Wiley, m c & m r: Stan Garrod, m l & b r: Australian Tourist Commission, b l: V. Last/Geographical Visual Aids; **p. 90:** t: Government of India Tourist Office, m l: Wiley Photo Files, m r & b: Stan Garrod; **p. 91:** t l: CIDA Photo/Patricio Baeza, t r: Japan National Tourist Organization, m r: Joe McNally/Sygma–Publiphoto, b l: Stan Garrod, b r: Gerry Gropp/Sipa Press–Publiphoto

Graph Credits

N. B.: Dates appearing in brackets are data collection years; other dates are date of publication.

Individual country information:
Population Figures (mid-1994): *1994 World Population Data Sheet* and additional information from Population Reference Bureau, Washington, D.C.;
Area Figures: *Philip's Geographical Digest 1992-3;*
Import/Export Figures: *Direction of Trade Statistics Yearbook, 1993,* International Monetary Fund;
Currency Information: Bank of America, 1994;
Main Languages: *Britannica Year Book 1993.*

Our graphs were created using the following sources:
p. 6: Ten Longest Rivers, Highest Points on Each Continent: *The New Encyclopedia Britannica,* 15th edition, 1987; **p. 7:** Area of the Continents: *Philip's Geographical Digest 1992-93;* **p. 8:** Ten Largest Nations, By Area (1992): *Philip's Geographical Digest 1992-93;* Ten Largest Nations, By Population and world population (mid-1994): *1994 World Population Data Sheet,* Population Reference Bureau; **p. 9:** World's Ten Largest Cities: *Statistical Abstract of the United States 1993, National Data Book;* **p. 12:** Percentage of World's Population (1990): *World Population Prospects 1990;* Percentage of World's Wealth: based on GNP figures from *Britannica Year Book 1993;* **p. 13:** Population Density: *Philip's Geographical Digest 1992-93; 1994 World Population Data Sheet;* **p. 14:** Major Earthquakes: *World Almanac and Book of Facts 1993;* **p. 22:** Mass of Seafood Caught (1990): *UN Statistical Yearbook 1990/91,* UN Publication 1993; **p. 26:** World Total Wood Use (1980): *Gaia: An Atlas of Planet Management,* 1984; **p. 27:** Forest Cover (1991), Forest Cover Change (1976-91): *FAO Production Yearbook 1992;* **p. 28:** Energy Imports and Exports (1990), Uranium Reserves (1990): *UN Statistical Yearbook 1990/91;* Energy Reserves, Coal, Natural Gas (1992), Crude Petroleum (1992): *Britannica Year Book 1993;* **p. 29:** Energy Consumption per Person (1990): *UN Statistical Yearbook 1990/91;* World Oil Demand: *Far Eastern Economic Review,* 14 Feb., 1991; **p. 32:** Male/Female Literacy Rates (1990): *UNESCO Yearbook 1992;* GDP per Person (1990): *World Almanac and Book of Facts 1993;* **p. 33:** Population Pyramids (1990): *The Age and Sex Distribution of the World Population, 1992 Revision,* UN Publication; **p. 34:** World's Shipping Fleet (1991): *Statistical Abstract of the United States 1993, National Data Book;* **p. 35:** Major Seaports of the Region (1991): *Shipping Statistics Yearbook 1992;* **p. 37:** Car Production (1990): *Philip's Geographical Digest 1992-93;* Imports and Exports (1991): *Europa World Year Book, 1993;* Trade Growth 1986-1992, Percentage of Trade (1992): *Direction of Trade Statistics Yearbook, 1993;* Major Trading Blocs: *The Globe and Mail, Classroom Edition,* December 1993; **p. 42:** Religions in Selected Countries (1992): *Britannica Year Book 1993;* **p. 45:** Major Languages in India (1992): *Britannica Year Book 1993;* **p. 51:** Population Pyramid (1990): *The Age and Sex Distribution of the World Population, 1992 Revision,* UN Publication; Import/Export Graphs (1989): *Europa World Year Book, 1993;* **p. 52:** Major Indonesian Crops (1991): *Europa World Year Book, 1993;* **p. 53:** Population Density: *Britannica Year Book 1993;* Land Use (1991): *FAO Production Yearbook 1992;* **p. 54:** Ethnic Groups (1990): *Philippines: A Country Study, 1993;* Religions (1992): *Britannica Year Book 1993;* **p. 55:** Ethnic Mix (1992), Import/Export Graphs (1991): *Europa World Year Book, 1993;* **p. 56:** Import/Export Graphs (1992): *Europa World Year Book, 1993;* **p. 57:** Trade per person (1992): *Direction of Trade Statistics Yearbook, 1993, 1994* and *World Population Data Sheet;* Percentage of Total World Trade: *The Globe and Mail,* April 7, 1994, sourced: GATT (1993); Top Ten Trading Nations (1992): *Direction of Trade Statistics Yearbook, 1993;* **p. 58:** Population Change: *World Population Prospects 1990;* **p. 59:** Urban/Rural Population: *World Development Reports,* World Bank (various); **p. 61:** Land Use (1991), Food Production (1991): *FAO Production Yearbook 1992;* **p. 64:** Population Percentage in Seoul: *Statistical Abstract of the United States 1993* and *Britannica Year Book 1993;* **p. 65:** Employment Distribution (1991): *UN Human Development Report, 1992;* Import/Export Graphs: *Europa World Year Book, 1993* and *Trade Statistics Yearbook, 1992;* Textile Exports, Ship Exports: *Trade Statistics Yearbook, 1992;* **p. 67:** Selected Products Manufactured (1992): *Europa World Year Book, 1993;* Land Use: *FAO Production Yearbook 1992;* **p. 70:** Employment Distribution in Japan (1991): *UN Human Development Report, 1992;* **p. 73:** Crop Production (1992): *Europa World Year Book, 1993;* Land Use (1990): *Britannica Year Book 1993;* **p. 74:** Population Changes: *Cat 93-301, A National Overview of Population & Dwelling Counts,* 1991 Census, Statistics Canada and *Cat 98-120 Canada's Population from Ocean to Ocean,* 1986 Census, Statistics Canada; **p. 75:** Imports/Exports (1991): *World Development Reports,* World Bank; **p. 78:** Population Changes: *Philip's Geographical Digest 1992-3;* **p. 79:** Import/Export Figures: *Statistical Abstract of the United States 1993;* **p. 82:** Population Density: *Philip's Geographical Digest 1992-93* and *1994 World Population Data Sheet;* Ethnic Groups: *Britannica Year Book 1993;* **p. 87:** Trading Partners (1990): *CIA World Databook 1991;* Goods Traded (1991): *World Development Reports,* World Bank; **p. 89:** Bauxite Producers (1989): *Europa World Year Book, 1993;* Land Use (1991): *FAO Production Yearbook 1992.*

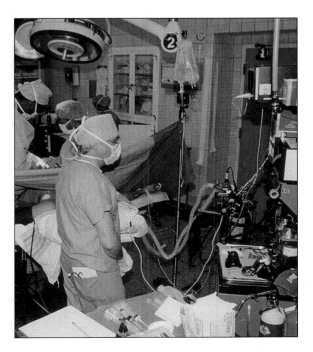

There are more than 40 independent countries located around the shores of the Pacific Ocean, and in the neighboring subcontinent of India. Together, they make up what we have come to call the "Pacific Rim".

A powerful unifying force has emerged among these nations: economic interdependence through trade, tourism, and economic cooperation. With more than 60% of the world's trade taking place within the Pacific Rim region, these countries represent the fastest-growing economic force in the world today.

The Pacific Rim Discovery Student Resource will help you explore the great physical and cultural diversity of the lands and peoples of the Pacific Rim. You will find that the region is home to two-thirds of the world's population and, as a result, is faced with great possibilities as well as challenges. Increasing trade, higher standards of living, and greater national wealth are having a beneficial effect on the citizens of many countries. Yet those same nations must still cope with problems such as population growth, environmental pollution, political conflict, and decreasing natural resources.

Each part of the enormous Pacific Rim region has a long and colorful history. You will examine some of the forces that have helped to shape the identity of these nations as you discover how great religions spread and empires rose and fell. Through maps and illustrations, you will follow the routes of explorers and traders. You will travel along the famous "Silk Road" and sail the sea-lanes of the legendary Spice Islands.

This book is neither a textbook nor an atlas in the traditional sense. It combines text, maps, photographs, illustrations, and graphs to provide you with an exciting, up-to-date view of an important part of our modern world. Most topics are presented in two-page spreads. As you explore them, you will not only learn about the lands and peoples of the Pacific Rim, you will also develop important skills in map reading, photograph interpretation, and the use of graphs, tables, and other statistical information. Perhaps, too, you will begin to think of the Pacific Rim, and of the world, in a different way.

A book like this can only begin to explore a region that is so vast. We hope that it will help you to understand the area, and will make you want to find out more about our neighbors around the Pacific.

Notes

Identifying Themes

Color bars at the top of each page identify very general themes for each page or spread in this resource. Blue appears on those pages that contain reference information, such as the Contents and Gazetteer. Pages that deal with "world" themes have green bars. All spreads that contain facts about the Pacific Rim as a region have gold at the top. Purple identifies pages that are devoted to specific countries, an area within a country, or a particular city.

Map Legends

Most maps in this resource have a box with a Legend explaining the different symbols, colors, and patterns used. Where a city is identified on a map, the size of its dot generally indicates the size of its population. The size of the type used for a city name can also reflect its size by population, especially since the symbols used for capital cities do not indicate size.

Abbreviations

B.C.E.: This is used to denote a particular year in history (e.g., 1500 B.C.E.) and means "Before the Common Era". This term replaces the label "B.C."

C.E.: This is also used to denote a particular year in history and means "Common Era". It replaces the label "A.D."

c.: This is a shortened form for "circa", which means "about", used with dates in history when the specific year is not known. An example of it in use is "Buddhism was founded in India c. 525 B.C.E."

Graph Abbreviations

Th: thousands; whatever figure appears before it must be multiplied by one thousand to determine the full numerical value.

M: millions; whatever figure appears before it must be multiplied by one million to determine the full numerical value.

B: billions; whatever figure appears before it must be multiplied by one billion to determine the full numerical value.

Contents

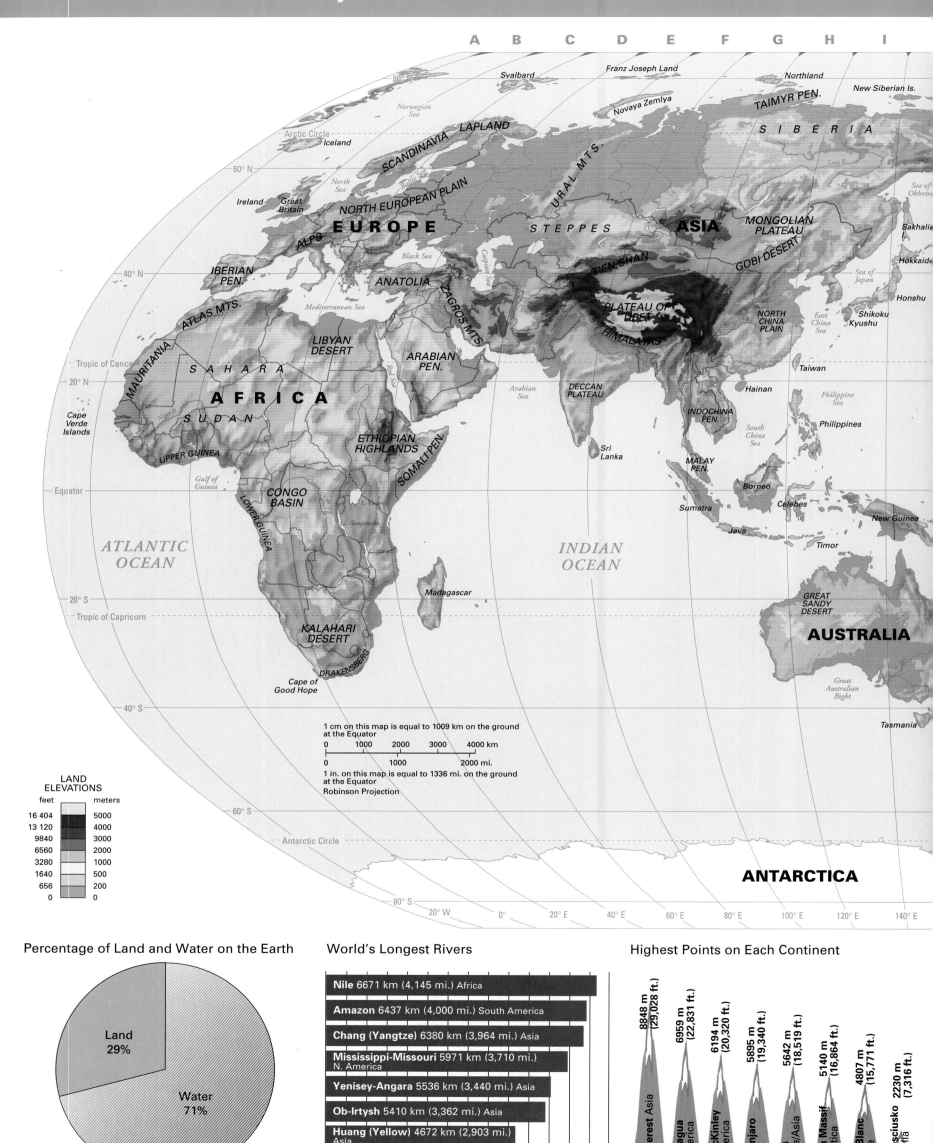

A B C D E F G H I

Svalbard · Franz Joseph Land · Northland · New Siberian Is.

Norwegian Sea · Novaya Zemlya · TAIMYR PEN. · S I B E R I A

Arctic Circle · Iceland · SCANDINAVIA · LAPLAND · URAL MTS.

60° N · North Sea · Baltic Sea · Sea of Okhotsk

Ireland · Great Britain · NORTH EUROPEAN PLAIN · S T E P P E S · ASIA · MONGOLIAN PLATEAU · Sakhalin

40° N · E U R O P E · Black Sea · Caspian Sea · TIEN SHAN · GOBI DESERT · Sea of Japan · Hokkaido

ALPS · IBERIAN PEN. · ANATOLIA · ZAGROS MTS. · PLATEAU OF TIBET · NORTH CHINA PLAIN · East China Sea · Honshu · Shikoku · Kyushu

ATLAS MTS. · Mediterranean Sea · HIMALAYAS

Tropic of Cancer · MAURITANIA · S A H A R A · LIBYAN DESERT · ARABIAN PEN. · Red Sea · Arabian Sea · DECCAN PLATEAU · Taiwan

20° N · A F R I C A · Hainan

Cape Verde Islands · S U D A N · ETHIOPIAN HIGHLANDS · SOMALI PEN. · Sri Lanka · INDOCHINA PEN. · Philippine Sea · Philippines

UPPER GUINEA · South China Sea

Gulf of Guinea · CONGO BASIN · LOWER GUINEA · MALAY PEN. · Borneo · Celebes

Equator · L. Victoria · Sumatra · New Guinea

Tanganyika · Java · Timor

ATLANTIC OCEAN · INDIAN OCEAN

20° S · Madagascar · GREAT SANDY DESERT

Tropic of Capricorn · AUSTRALIA

KALAHARI DESERT · DRAKENSBERG · Great Australian Bight

Cape of Good Hope

40° S · Tasmania

1 cm on this map is equal to 1009 km on the ground at the Equator

0 1000 2000 3000 4000 km

0 1000 2000 mi.

1 in. on this map is equal to 1336 mi. on the ground at the Equator
Robinson Projection

LAND ELEVATIONS

feet	meters
16 404	5000
13 120	4000
9840	3000
6560	2000
3280	1000
1640	500
656	200
0	0

60° S

Antarctic Circle

80° S · **ANTARCTICA**

20° W · 0° · 20° E · 40° E · 60° E · 80° E · 100° E · 120° E · 140° E

Percentage of Land and Water on the Earth

Land 29%

Water 71%

World's Longest Rivers

Nile 6671 km (4,145 mi.) Africa	
Amazon 6437 km (4,000 mi.) South America	
Chang (Yangtze) 6380 km (3,964 mi.) Asia	
Mississippi-Missouri 5971 km (3,710 mi.) N. America	
Yenisey-Angara 5536 km (3,440 mi.) Asia	
Ob-Irtysh 5410 km (3,362 mi.) Asia	
Huang (Yellow) 4672 km (2,903 mi.) Asia	

0 km 500 1000 1500 2000 2500 3000 3500 4000 4500 5000 5500 6000 6500 7000

Highest Points on Each Continent

Mt. Everest	8848 m (29,028 ft.)	Asia
Aconcagua	6959 m (22,831 ft.)	S. America
Mt. McKinley	6194 m (20,320 ft.)	N. America
Kilimanjaro	5895 m (19,340 ft.)	Africa
El'brus	5642 m (18,519 ft.)	Europe/Asia
Vinson Massif	5140 m (16,864 ft.)	Antarctica
Mont Blanc	4807 m (15,771 ft.)	Europe
Mt. Kosciusko	2230 m (7,316 ft.)	Australia

QUICK FACTS
Coldest place on earth: Plateau, Antarctica: average temp. = -56.7°C (-70°F)
Hottest place on earth: Dalol, Ethiopia: average temp. = 35°C (95°F)

7

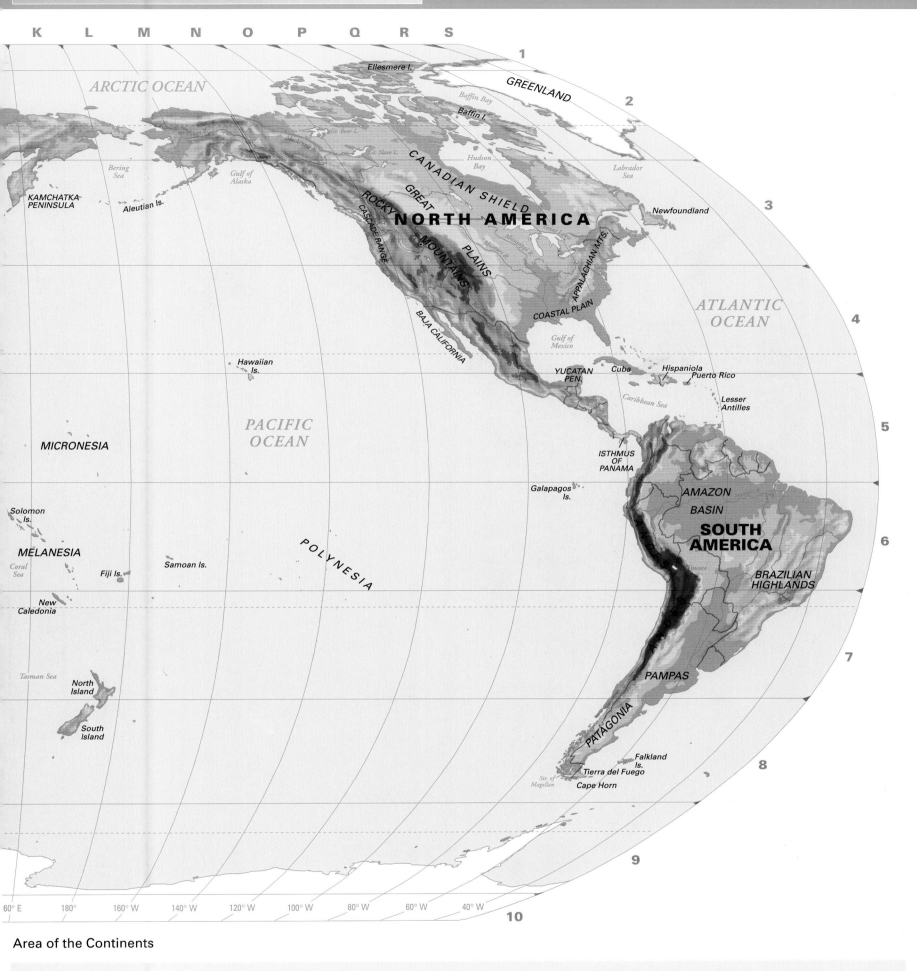

Area of the Continents

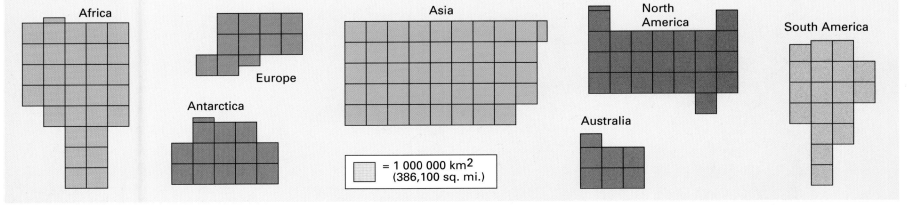

Africa

Asia

North America

Europe

South America

Antarctica

Australia

□ = 1 000 000 km² (386,100 sq. mi.)

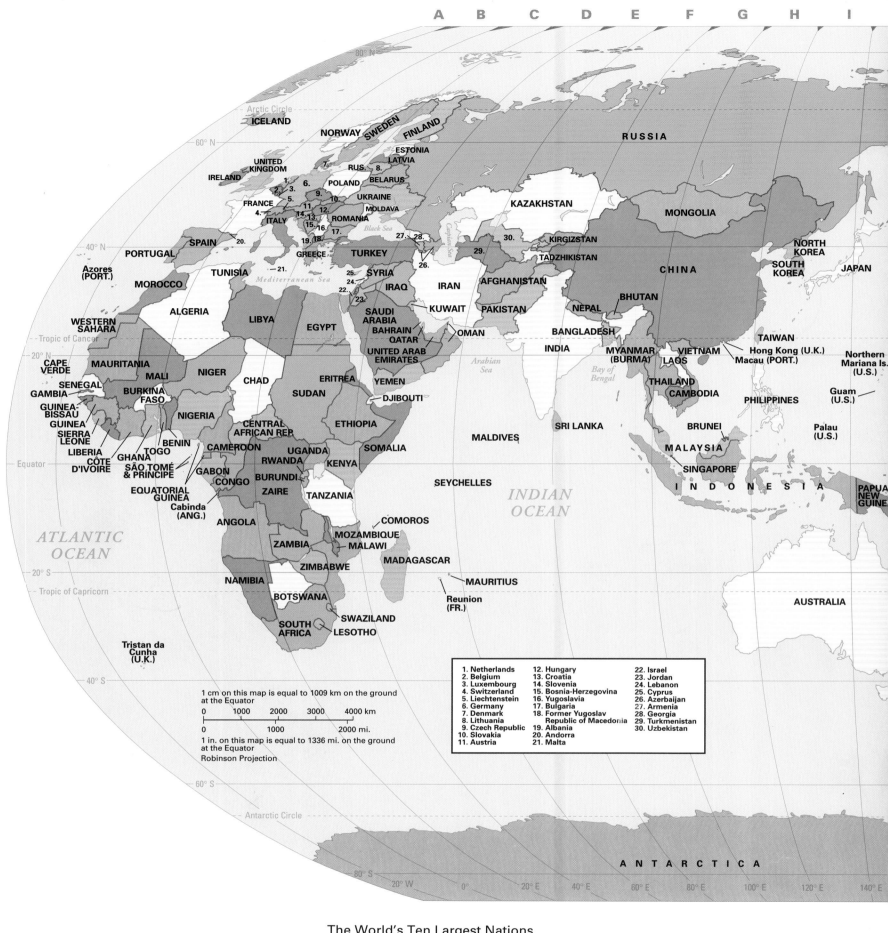

1 cm on this map is equal to 1009 km on the ground at the Equator

| 0 | 1000 | 2000 | 3000 | 4000 km |

| 0 | 1000 | 2000 mi. |

1 in. on this map is equal to 1336 mi. on the ground at the Equator
Robinson Projection

1. Netherlands	12. Hungary	22. Israel
2. Belgium	13. Croatia	23. Jordan
3. Luxembourg	14. Slovenia	24. Lebanon
4. Switzerland	15. Bosnia-Herzegovina	25. Cyprus
5. Liechtenstein	16. Yugoslavia	26. Azerbaijan
6. Germany	17. Bulgaria	27. Armenia
7. Denmark	18. Former Yugoslav	28. Georgia
8. Lithuania	Republic of Macedonia	29. Turkmenistan
9. Czech Republic	19. Albania	30. Uzbekistan
10. Slovakia	20. Andorra	
11. Austria	21. Malta	

The World's Ten Largest Nations

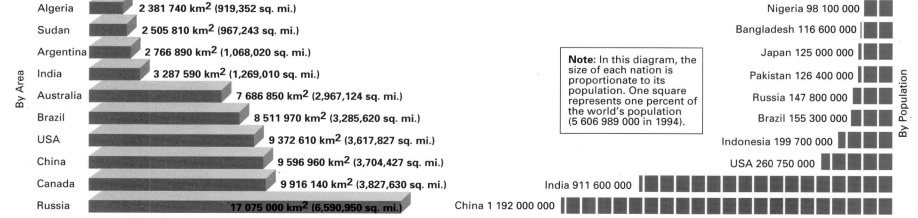

By Area

Algeria	2 381 740 km² (919,352 sq. mi.)
Sudan	2 505 810 km² (967,243 sq. mi.)
Argentina	2 766 890 km² (1,068,020 sq. mi.)
India	3 287 590 km² (1,269,010 sq. mi.)
Australia	7 686 850 km² (2,967,124 sq. mi.)
Brazil	8 511 970 km² (3,285,620 sq. mi.)
USA	9 372 610 km² (3,617,827 sq. mi.)
China	9 596 960 km² (3,704,427 sq. mi.)
Canada	9 916 140 km² (3,827,630 sq. mi.)
Russia	17 075 000 km² (6,590,950 sq. mi.)

Note: In this diagram, the size of each nation is proportionate to its population. One square represents one percent of the world's population (5 606 989 000 in 1994).

By Population

Nigeria	98 100 000
Bangladesh	116 600 000
Japan	125 000 000
Pakistan	126 400 000
Russia	147 800 000
Brazil	155 300 000
Indonesia	199 700 000
USA	260 750 000
India	911 600 000
China	1 192 000 000

QUICK FACTS Number of independent countries: 200
Number of languages spoken by more than 1 million people: 225
The first languages spoken by some of the world's population are: Mandarin 15%, Spanish 6%, English 6%, Bengali 3%.

9

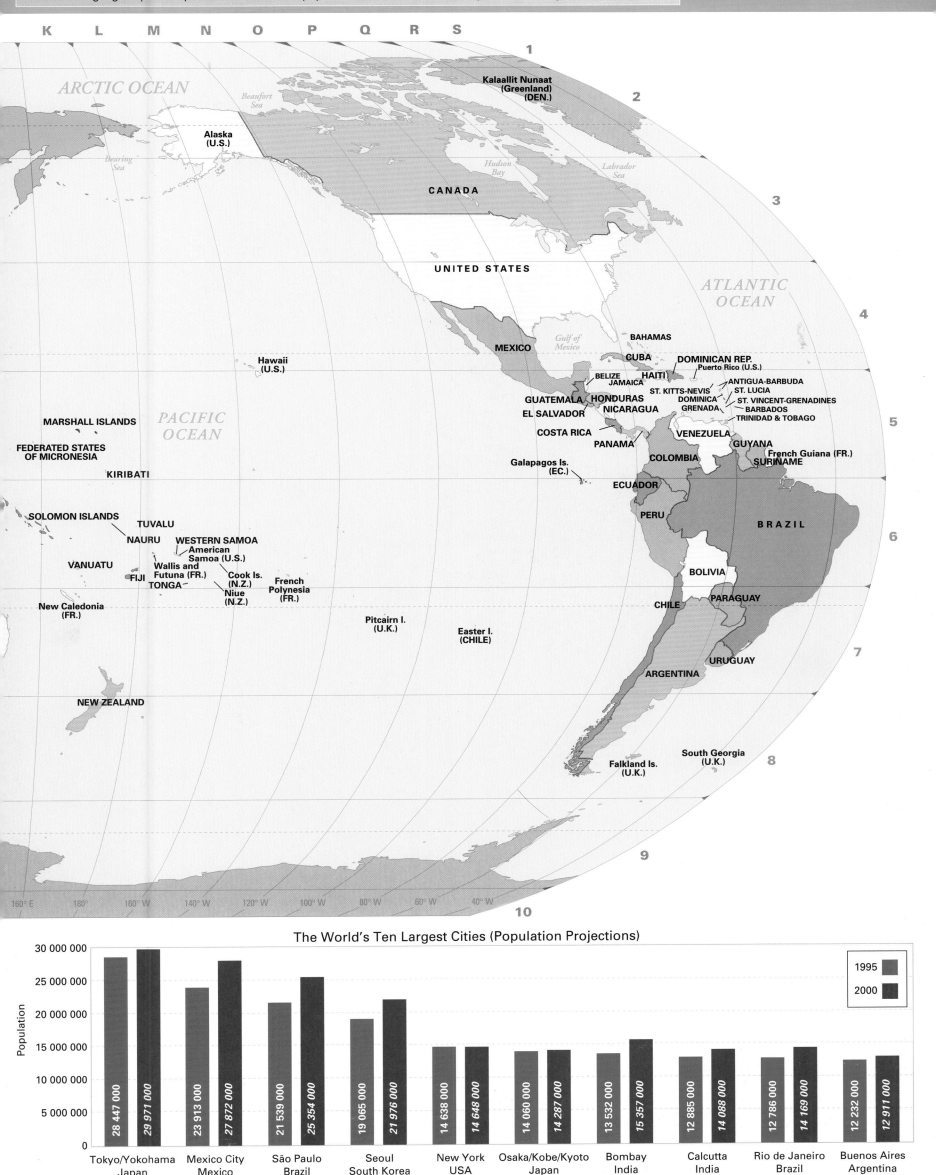

The World's Ten Largest Cities (Population Projections)

City	1995	2000
Tokyo/Yokohama Japan	28 447 000	29 971 000
Mexico City Mexico	23 913 000	27 872 000
São Paulo Brazil	21 539 000	25 354 000
Seoul South Korea	19 065 000	21 976 000
New York USA	14 638 000	14 648 000
Osaka/Kobe/Kyoto Japan	14 060 000	14 287 000
Bombay India	13 532 000	15 357 000
Calcutta India	12 885 000	14 088 000
Rio de Janeiro Brazil	12 786 000	14 169 000
Buenos Aires Argentina	12 232 000	12 911 000

10 Time Zones

If it's		then it's	
Thursday, 4:00 a.m. in Vancouver		Thursday, 7:00 p.m. in Bangkok	
Thursday, 2:00 a.m. in Honolulu		Thursday, 10:00 p.m. in Sydney	
Thursday, 6:00 p.m. in Honolulu		Friday, 2:00 p.m. in Sydney	

Standardizing Time

Until the 19th century, time was largely kept by the rising and setting of the sun. By the 20th century, increased travel and communications speeds made it necessary to divide the world into a set of organized time zones.

Time zones as we know them were invented in the late 19th century by a Canadian, Sir Sandford Fleming. He suggested that the world be divided into 24 time zones, one for each hour in the day. Moving from one zone to the next, an hour was either gained or lost. Fleming's idea was accepted throughout the world.

The International Date Line is an imaginary line that runs through the Pacific Ocean, generally at 180° longitude. Crossing this does not mean just gaining or losing an hour — it means gaining or losing an entire day. Traveling westward a day is lost…leave San Francisco early on Thursday morning, for example, and arrive in Tokyo on Friday morning. The opposite is true when traveling eastward.

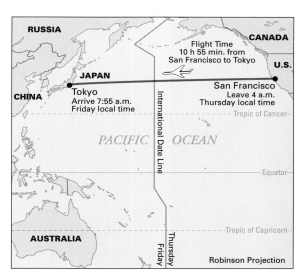

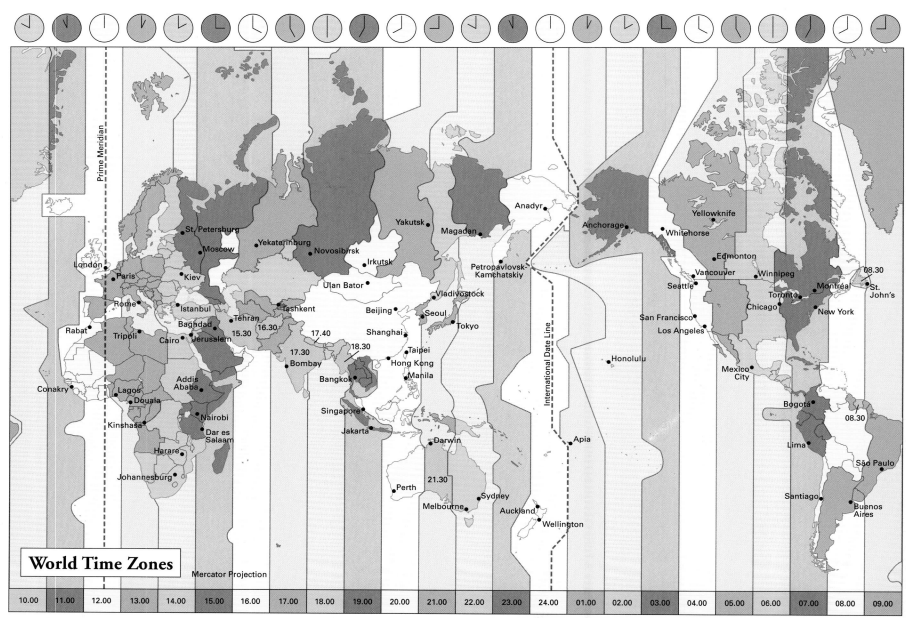

World Time Zones

Mercator Projection

| 10.00 | 11.00 | 12.00 | 13.00 | 14.00 | 15.00 | 16.00 | 17.00 | 18.00 | 19.00 | 20.00 | 21.00 | 22.00 | 23.00 | 24.00 | 01.00 | 02.00 | 03.00 | 04.00 | 05.00 | 06.00 | 07.00 | 08.00 | 09.00 |

As the earth rotates on its axis (an imaginary line joining the North and South Poles), half the world is in sunlight, while the other half is in darkness.

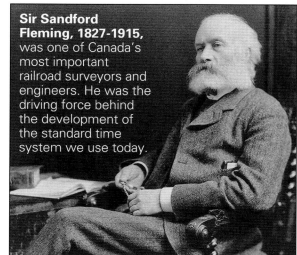

Sir Sandford Fleming, 1827–1915, was one of Canada's most important railroad surveyors and engineers. He was the driving force behind the development of the standard time system we use today.

Polar Projections

QUICK FACTS Ice covers about 98% of Antarctica.
Antarctica stores about 70% of the world's fresh water as ice.
Greenland is the world's largest island.

11

Mapping the Earth

Even though the earth is round, it can be mapped on a flat page in a number of different ways, called projections. Maps and the outlines of continents and countries can look very different depending on the particular map projection used.

The two maps on this page are polar projections, extending as far as the Equator in each. In one, the North Pole is at the center of the map. In the other, the South Pole is at the center.

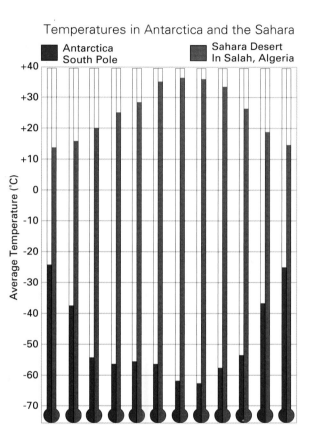

Temperatures in Antarctica and the Sahara

- ■ Antarctica South Pole
- ■ Sahara Desert In Salah, Algeria

There are enormous differences in temperature between Antarctica and the Sahara Desert. Precipitation, however, is so low in both areas that it is hard to measure.

Penguins, incredibly well-insulated birds, thrive in the harsh climate of Antarctica.

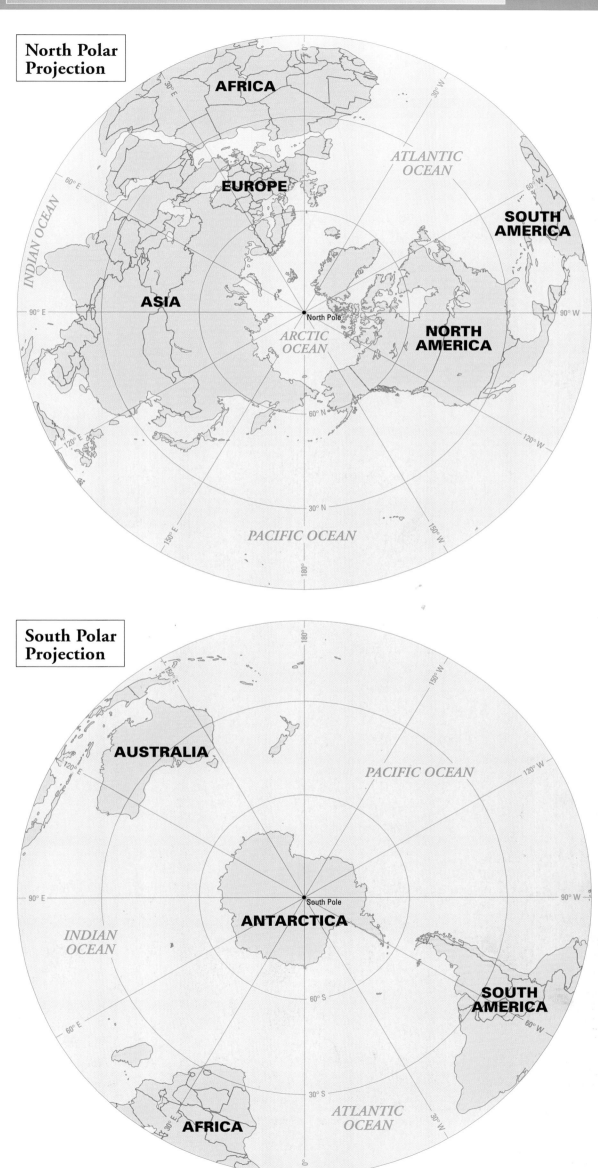

North Polar Projection

AFRICA

ATLANTIC OCEAN

EUROPE

INDIAN OCEAN

ASIA

SOUTH AMERICA

North Pole

ARCTIC OCEAN

NORTH AMERICA

PACIFIC OCEAN

South Polar Projection

AUSTRALIA

PACIFIC OCEAN

INDIAN OCEAN

South Pole

ANTARCTICA

SOUTH AMERICA

AFRICA

ATLANTIC OCEAN

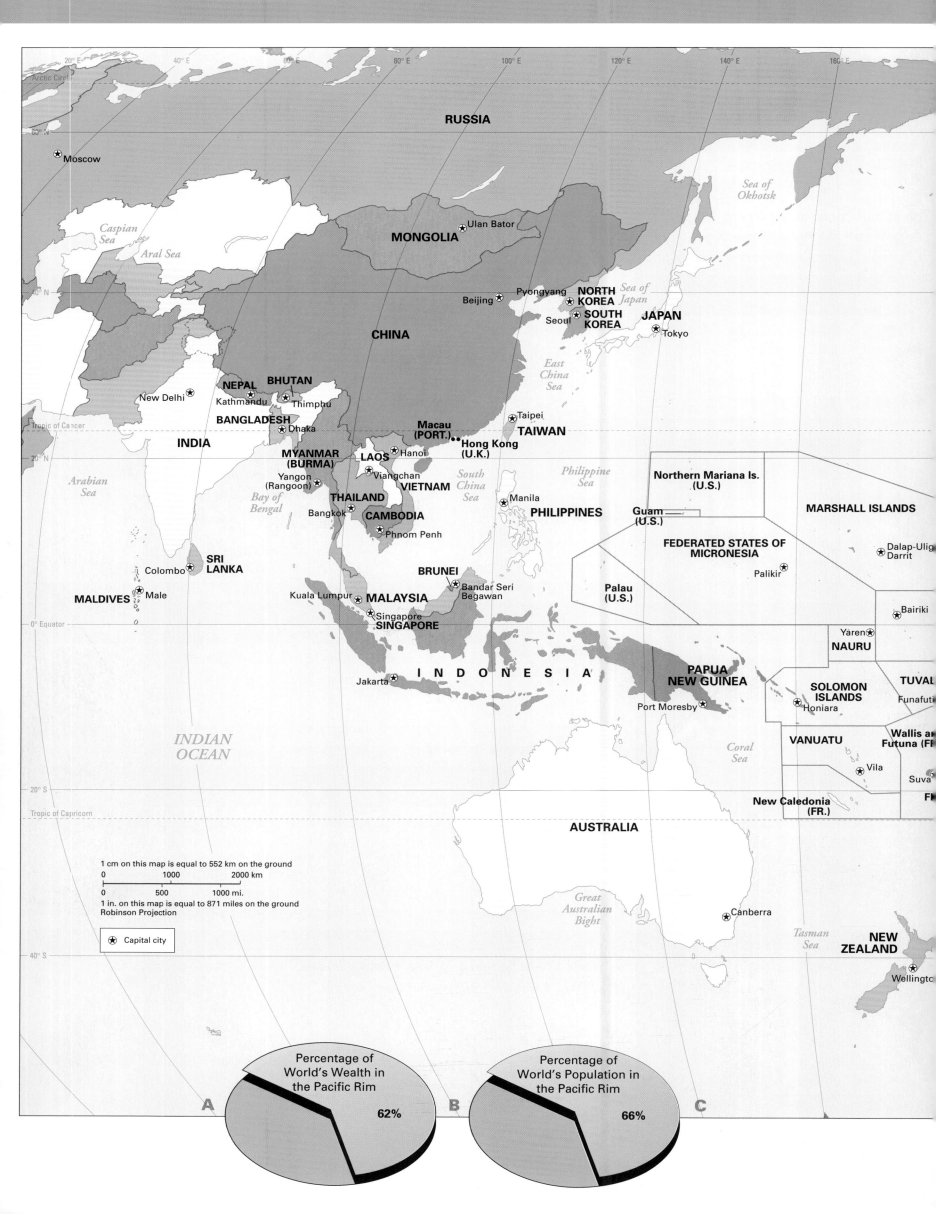

Percentage of World's Wealth in the Pacific Rim

62%

Percentage of World's Population in the Pacific Rim

66%

FLYING TIMES	from	Los Angeles	to	Hong Kong	14 h
		Los Angeles		Tokyo	11 h 15 min
		Vancouver		Tokyo	9 h 40 min
		Washington, D.C.		Hong Kong	19 h

Alaska
(U.S.)

Bering
Sea

Gulf of
Alaska

Hudson
Bay

CANADA

Labrador
Sea

Ottawa

UNITED STATES

Washington, D.C.

ATLANTIC
OCEAN

PACIFIC
OCEAN

Gulf of
Mexico

Hawaii
(U.S.)

MEXICO

Mexico City

BELIZE
Belmopan
GUATEMALA HONDURAS
Guatemala   Tegucigalpa
San Salvador   NICARAGUA
EL SALVADOR
Managua   San Jose
COSTA RICA   Panama
PANAMA

Caribbean Sea

Caracas

VENEZUELA

Bogota

COLOMBIA

Galapagos Is.
(EC.)

Quito

ECUADOR

BRAZIL

KIRIBATI

Tokelau
(N.Z.)

PERU

Lima

WESTERN
SAMOA

American
Samoa
(U.S.)

Apia

Cook
Islands
(N.Z.)

French Polynesia
(FR.)

La Paz

BOLIVIA

Sucre

PARAGUAY

Nuku'alofa   Niue
(N.Z.)
TONGA

Pitcairn
(U.K.)

Easter I.
(CHILE)

CHILE

Asuncion

E

F

URUGUAY
Montevideo

Santiago

Buenos Aires

ARGENTINA

ATLANTIC
OCEAN

G

Population Density of Selected Countries in the Pacific Rim

Country	Population Density	
	People/km²	People/sq. mi.
Australia	2.3	6.0
Canada	2.9	7.6
New Zealand	12.9	33.4
USA	27.8	72.0
Mexico	46.9	121.5
Thailand	115.8	299.9
China	124.2	321.8
North Korea	191.6	496.2
The Philippines	229.0	593.5
India	277.3	718.3
Japan	330.9	857.3
South Korea	448.9	1163.0
Taiwan	586.1	1518.0
Singapore	4725.8	12,259.4
Hong Kong	5622.1	14,544.8

Collision Zones

Because the Pacific basin is surrounded by a chain of volcanoes and earthquakes, scientists have named it the Rim of Fire.

The volcanoes and earthquakes of the Rim of Fire occur where different plates bump into, slide past, or separate from one another. A plate is a large section of the earth's crust that moves over a layer of hot, soft rock just below it. These plates move against one another along breaks in the crust called faults. Earthquakes are caused by this movement of crustal plates along faults. Volcanoes occur when molten rock from the earth's hot interior escapes through faults, cracks, and thin spots in the crust and breaks onto the earth's surface.

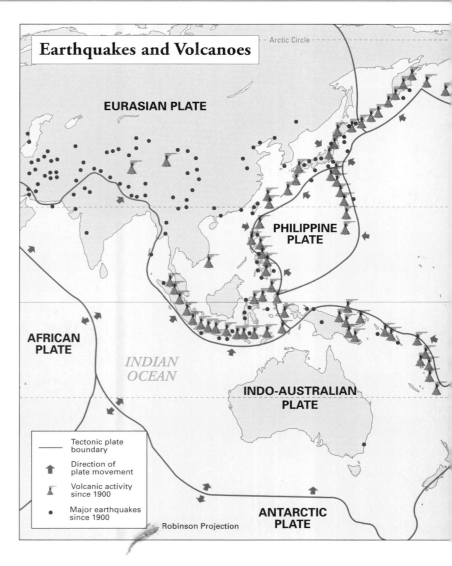

Earthquakes and Volcanoes

Because of their location near the San Andreas Fault, San Francisco and Los Angeles experience many earthquakes.

Loma Prieta is the official name of the San Francisco World Series earthquake of October 17, 1989. It measured 7.1 on the Richter scale — a very high reading. Sixty-three people died. There was over three billion dollars worth of property damage. The upper section of the San Francisco-Oakland Bay bridge snapped and collapsed onto the lower section during the earthquake. Miraculously, only one driver was killed.

Selected Major Earthquakes in the 20th Century

Location	Year	Richter Scale
San Francisco, USA	1906	8.3
Kansu, China	1920	8.6
Kansu, China	1932	7.6
Honshu, Japan	1946	8.4
Pelilio, Ecuador	1949	6.8
Southern Chile	1960	8.3
Northern Peru	1970	7.7
Mindanao, Philippines	1976	7.8
Sendai, Japan	1978	7.5
Colombia and Ecuador	1979	7.9
Honshu, Japan	1983	7.7
Mexico City, Mexico	1985	8.1
San Francisco, USA	1989	7.1
Luzon, Philippines	1990	7.7
Yucca Valley, USA	1992	7.4
Los Angeles, USA	1994	6.6

Richter Scale 0 1 2 3 4 5 6 7 8 9

QUICK FACTS   Most people killed in an earthquake: 830 000; Shaanxi, China, Jan. 24, 1556
Earthquake with highest Richter scale reading: 8.9, Japan, March 2, 1933; 2990 people killed
Most earthquakes each year: Japanese islands; about 1500 annually

15

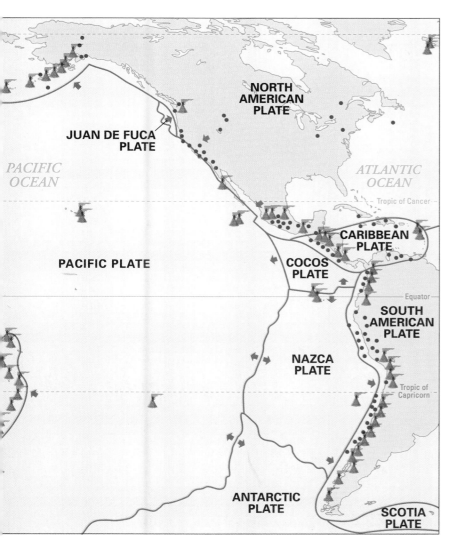

Composite volcanoes are made up of layers of ash and lava. They are steeply sloped.

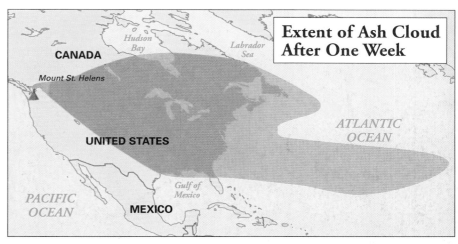

▶ Mount St. Helens erupted in 1980. It had been inactive for 450 years. The force of the eruption was 500 times greater than the Hiroshima atom bomb. It reduced the height of the mountain by 385 m (1,267 ft.).

Composite volcanoes produce thick ash when they erupt and are sometimes called cinder volcanoes for this reason.

Extent of Ash Cloud After One Week

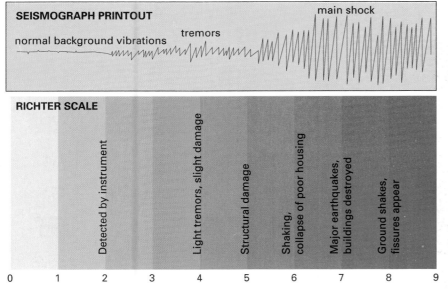

SEISMOGRAPH PRINTOUT

normal background vibrations   tremors   main shock

RICHTER SCALE

0	1	2	3	4	5	6	7	8	9

Detected by instrument

Light tremors, slight damage

Structural damage

Shaking, collapse of poor housing

Major earthquakes, buildings destroyed

Ground shakes, fissures appear

Readings recorded on a seismograph enable scientists to determine the strength of an earthquake. The strength of an earthquake is measured on the Richter scale.

Shield volcanoes, like those in Hawaii, produce mostly lava. They are gently sloped.

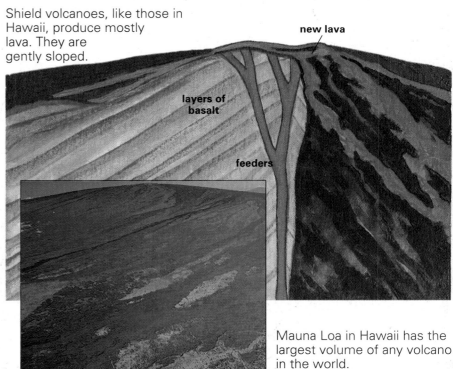

Mauna Loa in Hawaii has the largest volume of any volcano in the world.

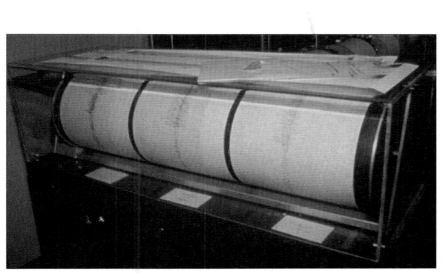

A Mountainous Region

Many of the lands of the Pacific Rim are mountainous. Some mountains, such as the Rocky Mountains and the Himalayas, are "young" mountains. They rise to dramatic snow-capped heights thousands of meters above sea level. Other mountains are much older. Their once tall peaks have been eroded through the action of glacial ice, water, and wind.

Most of the mountains in the region were formed along the boundaries of crustal plates by volcanic activity, folding, and faulting.

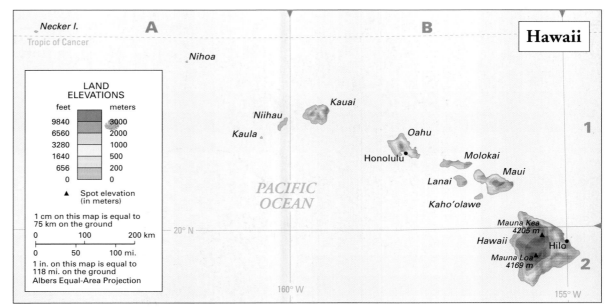

Plates move only a few centimeters each year. When they collide, the force is enormous. It is strong enough that, over time, one plate can be pushed up thousands of meters along the fault line. In this way, some mountains are formed.

Hawaii is made up of a chain of volcanic islands. They rise from the floor of the Pacific Ocean to heights between 7000-10 000 m (23,000-33-000ft.). Each island is the upper portion of a shield volcano.

▶ The Coast Mountains of British Columbia are volcanic in origin, but were pushed up by faulting.

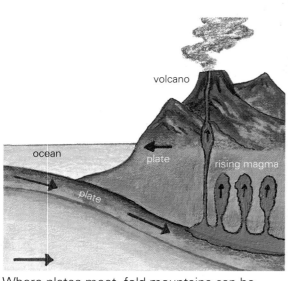

Where plates meet, fold mountains can be formed when the heavier ocean plate is pushed downwards into the hot interior of the earth while the lighter continental plate is bent, or folded, upwards.

When tectonic plates cause the earth's crust to buckle, large sections of the crust rise into the air and form rugged mountain ranges.

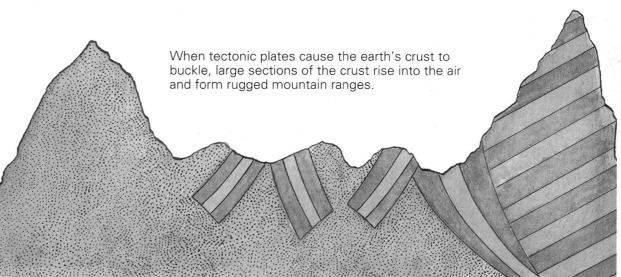

QUICK FACTS   Mount Paricutin in Mexico is only about fifty years old.
The world's tallest mountain measured from the sea floor to its peak is Mauna Kea: 10 208 m (33,490 ft.).
The highest unclimbed mountain is Namcha Barwa in China: 7782 m (25,531 ft.).

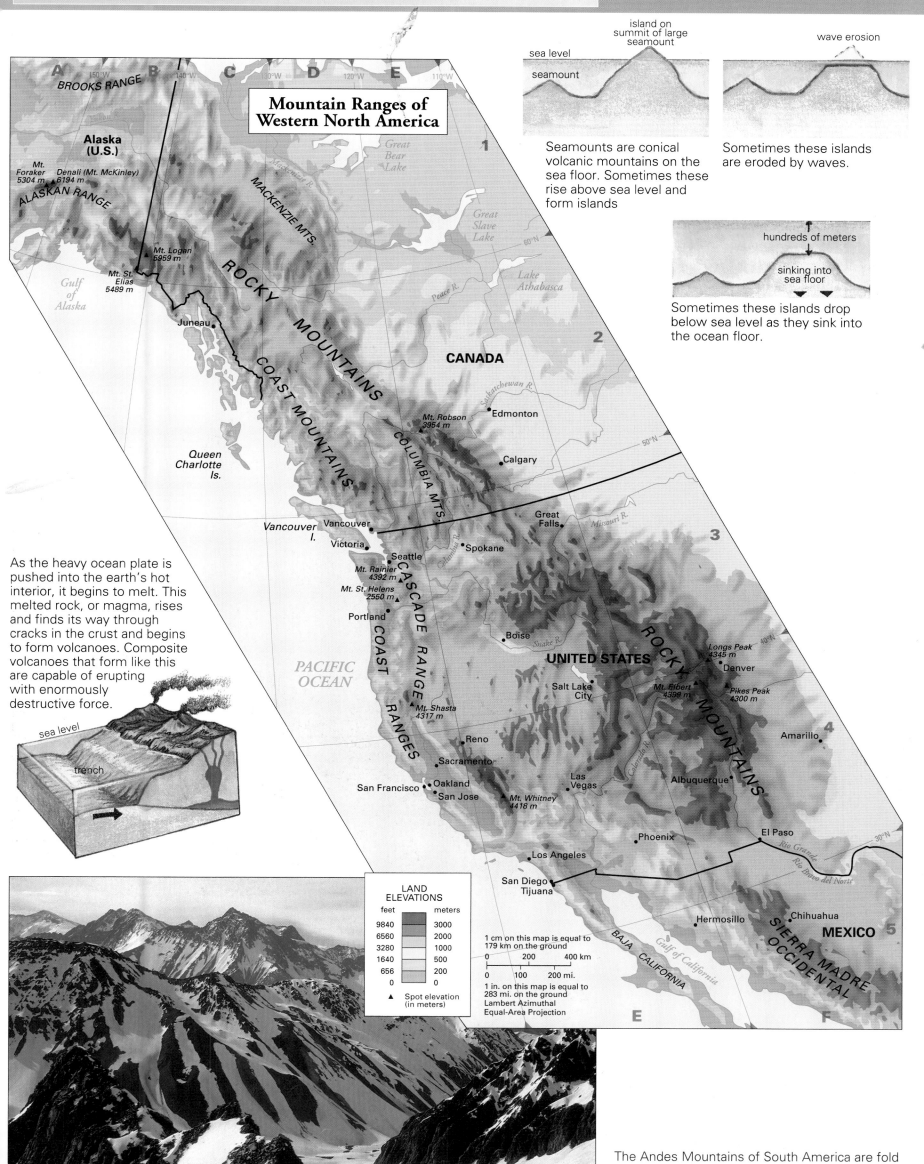

Mountain Ranges of Western North America

Seamounts are conical volcanic mountains on the sea floor. Sometimes these rise above sea level and form islands

Sometimes these islands are eroded by waves.

Sometimes these islands drop below sea level as they sink into the ocean floor.

As the heavy ocean plate is pushed into the earth's hot interior, it begins to melt. This melted rock, or magma, rises and finds its way through cracks in the crust and begins to form volcanoes. Composite volcanoes that form like this are capable of erupting with enormously destructive force.

LAND ELEVATIONS

feet	meters
9840	3000
6560	2000
3280	1000
1640	500
656	200
0	0

▲ Spot elevation (in meters)

1 cm on this map is equal to 179 km on the ground

0   200   400 km

0   100   200 mi.

1 in. on this map is equal to 283 mi. on the ground
Lambert Azimuthal Equal-Area Projection

The Andes Mountains of South America are fold mountains that include many volcanoes.

Ocean Currents: Rivers in the Oceans

The waters of the world's oceans and seas are constantly moving. Waves rolling in on a sandy beach or rocky headland are a common example of ocean waters in motion.

Less easily seen, but much bigger, are the movements known as ocean currents. These currents are like huge rivers, within the oceans, that carry massive amounts of water. They influence the lives of all sea-dwelling plants and animals as well as the climates of coastal areas on all continents. In the past, they were also important influences on the routes of explorers.

The energy that powers ocean currents comes from the winds that pass over the surface of the water. The direction and strength of the winds and the position of continents determine the direction of flow and the strength of ocean currents. When winds change direction from season to season, they also change the ocean currents.

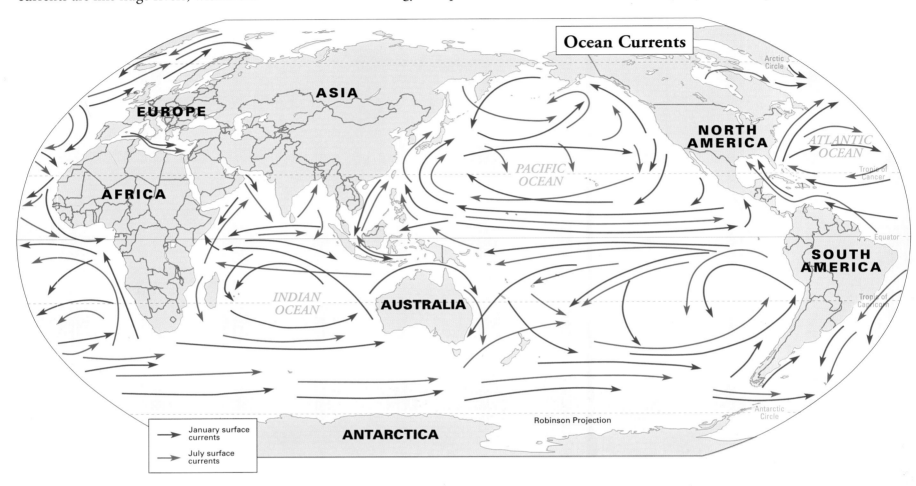

Ocean Currents

ASIA

EUROPE

NORTH AMERICA

ATLANTIC OCEAN

AFRICA

PACIFIC OCEAN

Arctic Circle

Tropic of Cancer

Equator

SOUTH AMERICA

INDIAN OCEAN

AUSTRALIA

Tropic of Capricorn

Antarctic Circle

ANTARCTICA

Robinson Projection

→ January surface currents

→ July surface currents

Winds are currents of moving air that are caused by differences in air pressure. Winds always move from areas with higher air pressure to those with lower air pressure. As winds move over an ocean's surface, they transfer some of their energy to the water. This energy is what drives ocean currents.

Creating Ocean Currents

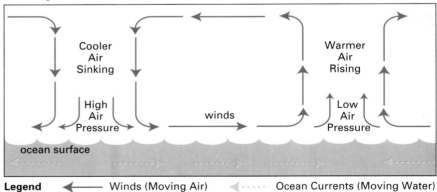

Cooler Air Sinking

High Air Pressure

winds

Warmer Air Rising

Low Air Pressure

ocean surface

Legend ◄— Winds (Moving Air) ◄---- Ocean Currents (Moving Water)

Normal Conditions

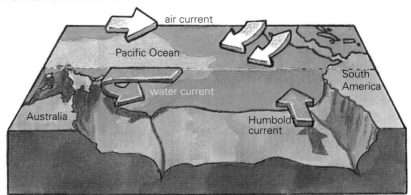

air current

Pacific Ocean

water current

South America

Australia

Humboldt current

Ocean currents have a tremendous influence on fish and other marine wildlife. Changes in these currents can sometimes kill off millions of these animals, causing too, great hardship for many people who depend on fishing for their livelihoods.

In normal years, the trade winds push warm Pacific water westward. This allows cool, nutrient-rich water to upwell to replace it. When the warm water reaches Indonesia, it forms a large pool of warm water.

QUICK FACTS
Scientists cannot prove what causes El Niño events.

El Niño ("The Child") was so named because it appears near Christmas. The 1991-1994 El Niño event was the longest this century.

19

El Niño: The Pacific's Problem Child

Every four or five years, usually in December, the prevailing winds of the Pacific are overpowered by winds pushing eastwards. This causes a warm ocean current to flow back toward South America; this current, under these conditions, is called El Niño. The changes that may result from this abnormal current can be drastic. Some parts may experience drought, while others receive heavy rains that cause flooding. As well, in the southern Pacific, typhoon tracks may change.

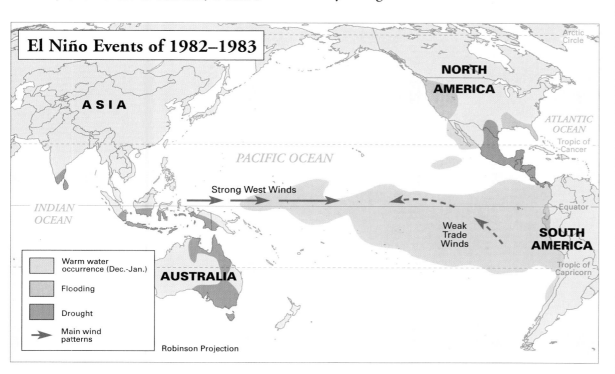

El Niño Events of 1982–1983

Legend:
- Warm water occurrence (Dec.-Jan.)
- Flooding
- Drought
- Main wind patterns

Robinson Projection

Heavy rains caused by an El Niño event in 1992 caused severe flooding in Texas.

El Niño Conditions

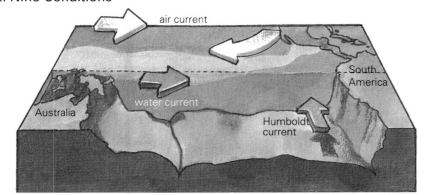

In El Niño years, this is reversed because the winds from the west become stronger. The winds drive the warm water eastward toward the coast of South America.

▶ In March, 1983, southeast Australia was hit by its most severe drought in years. The suspected cause was an El Niño event. The lives of 40 million sheep and 5 million head of cattle were put in danger.

Results of the 1982-83 El Niño Event

Continent	Unusual Events
Australia/Oceania	Australia suffered its worst drought in 200 years. Six tropical typhoons devastated Tahiti in less than six months.
Asia	The monsoon wind system failed to develop in Indonesia and the Philippines. This resulted in crop failure and food shortages.
South America	Heavy rains fell in normally dry areas. Flood damage was very widespread. Commercial fishing was disrupted. Many people lost their livelihoods.
North America	Abnormally heavy winter and spring rains caused the worst flooding in decades in the mid-west and south. In the north central region, winter temperatures were the warmest in 25 years. This reduced corn and soybean harvests. Coastal storms in California caused mudslides and flooding. Damage was over a billion dollars.

Monsoons

Monsoons are seasonal winds. The yearly monsoon cycle helps create the climate of much of Asia. In the winter, cold dry winds flow out of central Asia. In the summer, warm moist winds blow from the Pacific and Indian Oceans onto the land. In many Asian countries, farmers plant and harvest according to the seasons created by the monsoons.

Water is a scarce and important resource in the dry season, as these signs in Australia show.

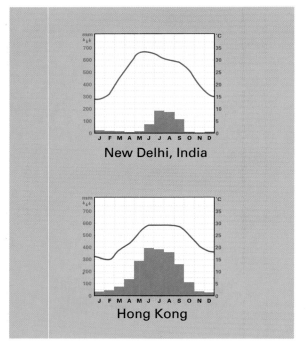

New Delhi, India

Hong Kong

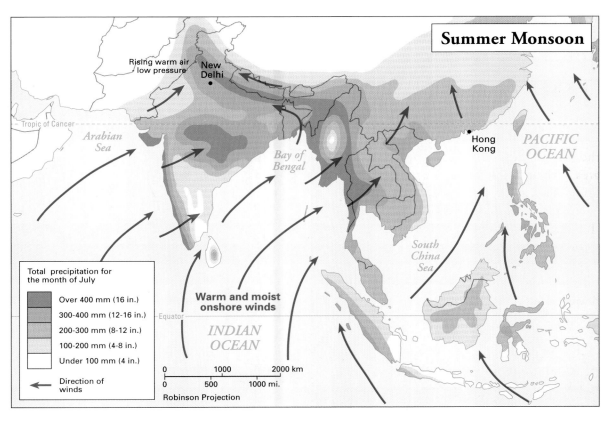

Summer Monsoon

Rising warm air low pressure — New Delhi

Tropic of Cancer

Arabian Sea

Bay of Bengal

Hong Kong

PACIFIC OCEAN

South China Sea

Warm and moist onshore winds

Equator

INDIAN OCEAN

Total precipitation for the month of July

- Over 400 mm (16 in.)
- 300-400 mm (12-16 in.)
- 200-300 mm (8-12 in.)
- 100-200 mm (4-8 in.)
- Under 100 mm (4 in.)
- ← Direction of winds

| 0 | 1000 | 2000 km |
| 0 | 500 | 1000 mi. |

Robinson Projection

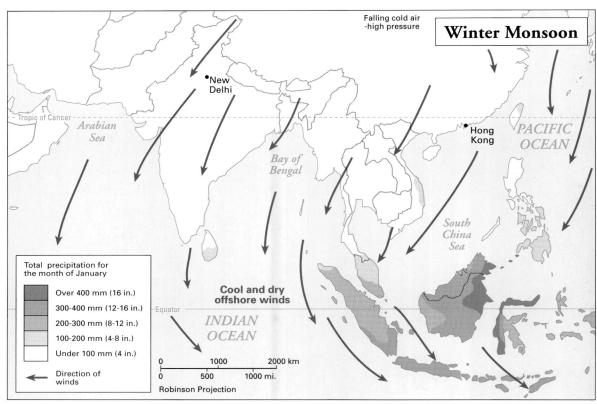

Falling cold air -high pressure

Winter Monsoon

New Delhi

Tropic of Cancer

Arabian Sea

Hong Kong

PACIFIC OCEAN

Bay of Bengal

South China Sea

Cool and dry offshore winds

Equator

INDIAN OCEAN

Total precipitation for the month of January

- Over 400 mm (16 in.)
- 300-400 mm (12-16 in.)
- 200-300 mm (8-12 in.)
- 100-200 mm (4-8 in.)
- Under 100 mm (4 in.)
- ← Direction of winds

| 0 | 1000 | 2000 km |
| 0 | 500 | 1000 mi. |

Robinson Projection

An abundance of water is needed for rice cultivation.

Even during the dry season, agricultural activities take place.

QUICK FACTS

1990: typhoon Mike caused 190 deaths in the Philippines
1992: monsoon floods caused more than 1000 deaths in China

World's heaviest annual rainfall: Kauai, Hawaii; 1168 cm (460 in.)
India's rainfall: 75% is from monsoons

21

Tropical Cyclones and Typhoons

Tropical cyclones are intense storms that can have winds of more than 160 km/h (100 mph). They are accompanied by heavy rain and thunder. The winds revolve around the "eye of the storm". The eye is the calm area at the storm's center. It can be up to 20 km (12.5 mi.) across.

Typhoon is the name given to cyclones in the western Pacific and South China Sea. (A typhoon is the same as a hurricane.) Typhoons generally occur from early August till the end of October, often causing great devastation.

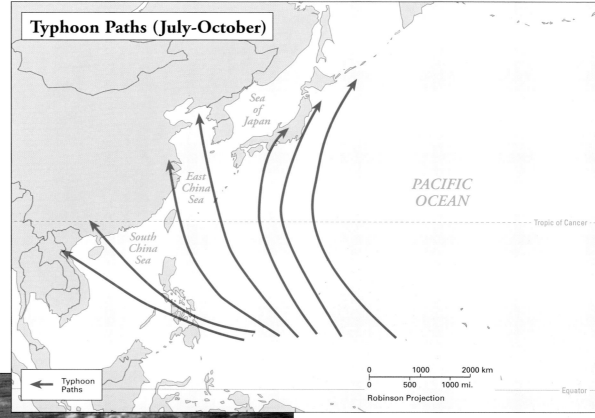

Typhoon Paths (July-October)

A Space View of a Typhoon Forming Over the South Pacific Ocean

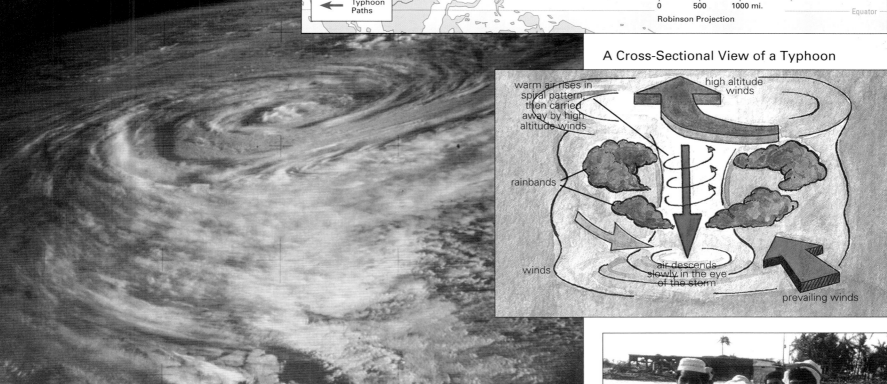

Tropical cyclones move across the water and often cause great flooding and damage when they reach the land.

A Cross-Sectional View of a Typhoon

warm air rises in spiral pattern, then carried away by high altitude winds

high altitude winds

rainbands

winds

air descends slowly in the eye of the storm

prevailing winds

The Pacific Ocean: A Resource in Danger

The Pacific Ocean, the largest water body in the world, covers one-third of the earth's surface. It provides the livelihood for millions of people. Each year, millions of tonnes of fish, shellfish, and edible seaweed are taken from the ocean. Oil, metals, and minerals are taken from under the ocean.

There are, however, serious problems. As the population of Pacific Rim countries grows, the ocean is increasingly abused. More and more human, agricultural, and industrial waste is dumped in it. Resources are being overharvested. All of these activities threaten the existence of the Pacific Ocean's rich marine environments.

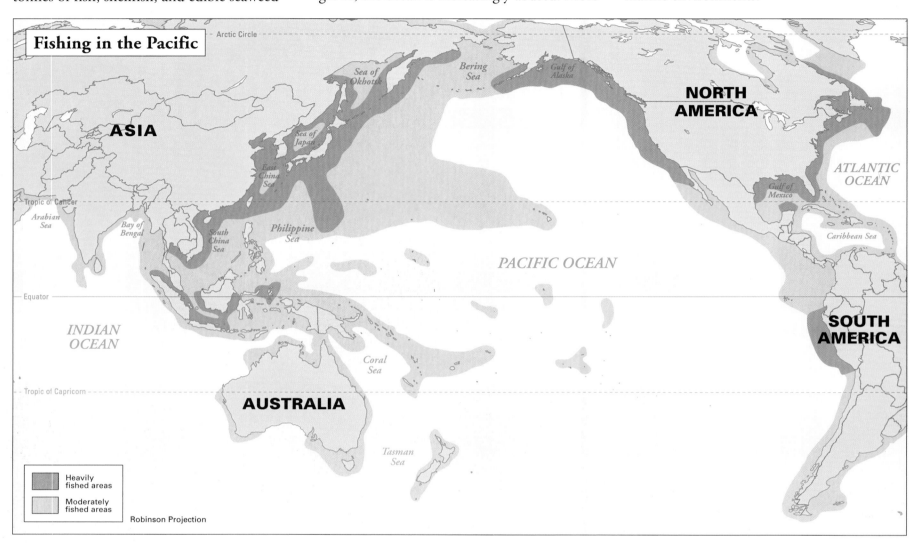

Fishing in the Pacific

ASIA

NORTH AMERICA

ATLANTIC OCEAN

PACIFIC OCEAN

INDIAN OCEAN

SOUTH AMERICA

AUSTRALIA

Legend:
- Heavily fished areas
- Moderately fished areas

Robinson Projection

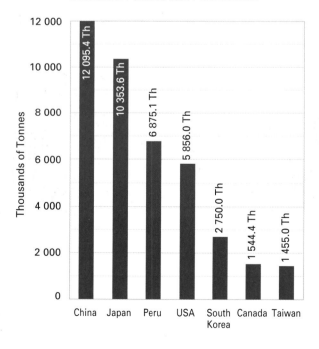

Mass of All Seafood Caught by Selected Pacific Rim Countries

- China: 12 095.4 Th
- Japan: 10 353.6 Th
- Peru: 6 875.1 Th
- USA: 5 856.0 Th
- South Korea: 2 750.0 Th
- Canada: 1 544.4 Th
- Taiwan: 1 455.0 Th

(Thousands of Tonnes)

Seiners catch fish by enclosing them in huge nets. Because they catch so many fish, there is a danger that stocks will die off.

Many fishing communities around the Pacific Rim have local fish markets.

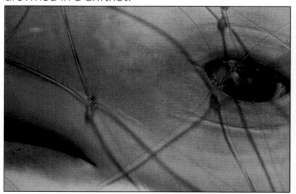

This white-sided dolphin suffered the same fate as many other species of marine life — drowned in a driftnet.

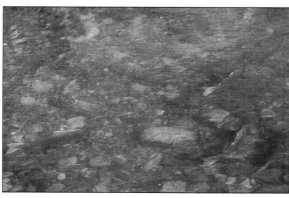

▶ Five species of salmon mature in the northern Pacific. They then return to the streams in which they were born in North America and Asia. Here, they spawn and die. Pacific salmon are of great economic benefit to Canada, the United States, and Japan.

QUICK FACTS

Area of Pacific Ocean: 165 250 000 km² (63,800,000 sq. mi.)
Greatest Depth: 11 034 m (36,200 ft.)

Area of Atlantic Ocean: 82 440 000 km² (31,830,000 sq. mi.)
Greatest Depth: 9219 m (30,246 ft.)

23

Ocean Zones

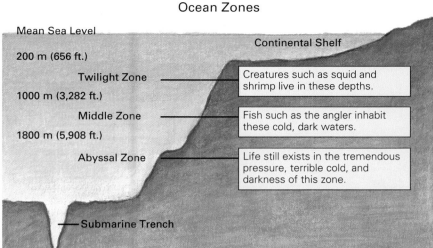

Mean Sea Level

200 m (656 ft.)

Continental Shelf

Twilight Zone — Creatures such as squid and shrimp live in these depths.

1000 m (3,282 ft.)

Middle Zone — Fish such as the angler inhabit these cold, dark waters.

1800 m (5,908 ft.)

Abyssal Zone — Life still exists in the tremendous pressure, terrible cold, and darkness of this zone.

— Submarine Trench

Oil spilled by tankers is devastating to birds and marine life. Clean-up operations are costly and time-consuming, but essential.

The Deep Sea Trenches

Very deep submarine trenches occur in the Pacific. They form at the edges of continental slopes and island arcs such as the Japanese Archipelago. The Mariana Trench in the western Pacific is the lowest known point on earth's surface. It reaches 11 034 m (36,200 ft.) below sea level.

Special ships, such as this deep ocean research vessel, explore for minerals.

▼ Oil companies use oil rigs to tap into the vast wealth of petroleum reserves beneath the ocean's floor. Leakage of oil from these rigs kills fish and sea birds and severely damages marine environments.

Ocean-Floor Resources

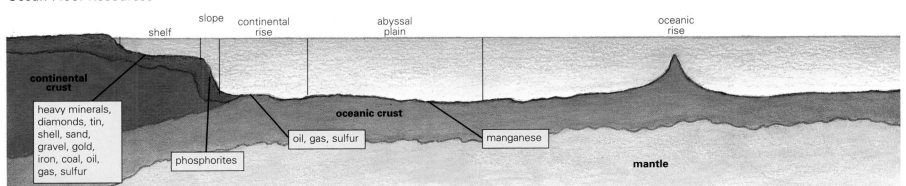

shelf
slope
continental rise
abyssal plain
oceanic rise

continental crust

oceanic crust

heavy minerals, diamonds, tin, shell, sand, gravel, gold, iron, coal, oil, gas, sulfur

phosphorites

oil, gas, sulfur

manganese

mantle

Animals and Their Habitats

Almost every type of habitat, from cold desert to tropical rainforest, is found in the Pacific Rim area. An astonishing variety of wildlife, including rare species such as the Javan rhino and the giant panda, inhabits the region.

Here as elsewhere, human activities threaten natural habitats. Wildlife has come under increasing pressure, and many species are on the verge of extinction. Sadly, many more are already extinct.

Habitats are destroyed to make way for urban, industrial, and agricultural development. Once their nesting, breeding, and feeding places are gone, whole populations of animals and plants disappear.

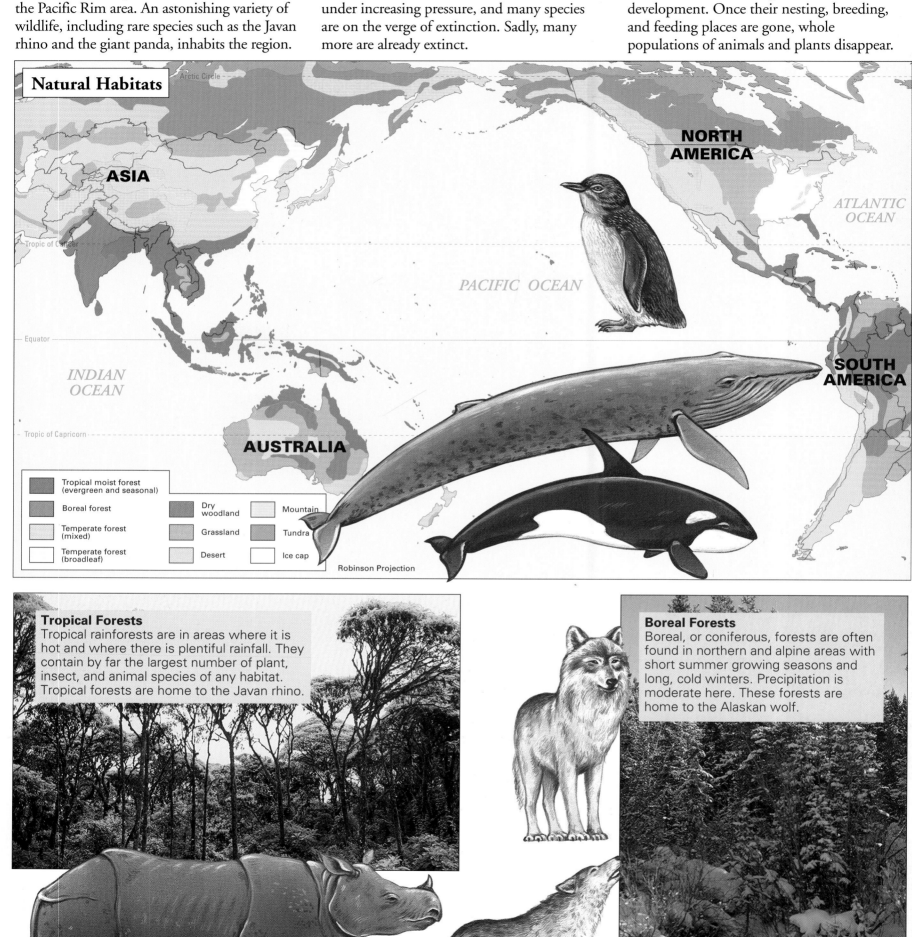

Natural Habitats

NORTH AMERICA

ASIA

ATLANTIC OCEAN

PACIFIC OCEAN

INDIAN OCEAN

SOUTH AMERICA

AUSTRALIA

Tropical moist forest (evergreen and seasonal)

Boreal forest

Temperate forest (mixed)

Temperate forest (broadleaf)

Dry woodland

Grassland

Desert

Mountain

Tundra

Ice cap

Robinson Projection

Tropical Forests

Tropical rainforests are in areas where it is hot and where there is plentiful rainfall. They contain by far the largest number of plant, insect, and animal species of any habitat. Tropical forests are home to the Javan rhino.

Boreal Forests

Boreal, or coniferous, forests are often found in northern and alpine areas with short summer growing seasons and long, cold winters. Precipitation is moderate here. These forests are home to the Alaskan wolf.

Note: Animals are not drawn to scale.

QUICK FACTS
Estimated number of species in the world: 3 to 80 million   Rarest large animal: Javan rhinoceros
Estimated number of species identified: 1.5 million   Panda's diet: 18 kg (40 lb.) of bamboo daily

25

Mixed Temperate Forests
Mixed temperate forests contain deciduous and coniferous trees. Asian highland forests are home to the panda, which feeds on bamboo.

Grasslands
Grasslands are areas with widely spaced trees and tall grasses between them. They occur where there are one or two wet seasons separated by long dry periods. Grasslands in North America are home to the bison.

Mountain
Vegetation in a mountain region varies widely. It depends upon the climate, which is influenced by altitude and latitude. The Himalayas of Asia are home to the snow leopard.

Drylands
Drylands and deserts can have droughts that may last for several years. Plants are few, but if rain falls, the drylands can "bloom". Drylands in North America are home to the tortoise and many other animals.

Endangered Species

orangutan

Well over 99% of all species that have ever lived have disappeared. Because of human activities, the extinction rate has soared. Between 50 and 100 species disappear every day from the earth. The animals pictured here are endangered, except the Tasmanian wolf, which is already extinct.

Tasmanian wolf, or tiger

tapir

Tundra
Tundra is a cold, semi-desert region. The land remains snow-bound for up to eight months of the year. Tundra is home to the Arctic lemming.

A Renewable Resource

Forests are important both to natural ecosystems and to human economic systems.

The world's forests play a major role in the production of oxygen. They are home to millions of species of plants and animals.

Forests also affect rainfall, temperature, and other climatic conditions.

Many thousands of workers from Chile to Tasmania earn their living in the forest industry. Thousands more are employed making pulp and paper and wood products.

Wood products from the forests are used to build homes, make tools, create furniture and art, heat homes, and cook food.

In order to preserve our forests for the future, we must use them with great care. All people are responsible for this precious resource.

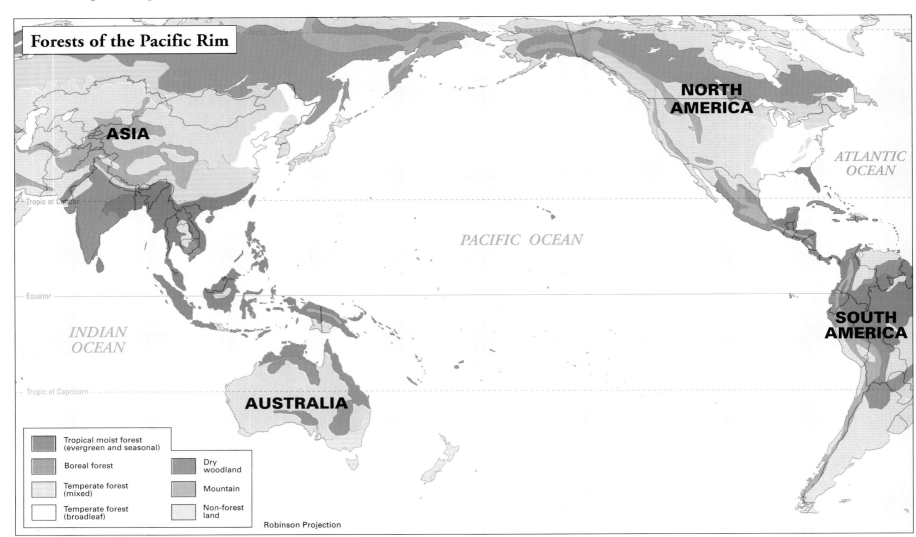

Forests of the Pacific Rim

ASIA
NORTH AMERICA
ATLANTIC OCEAN
PACIFIC OCEAN
INDIAN OCEAN
SOUTH AMERICA
AUSTRALIA

Tropic of Cancer
Equator
Tropic of Capricorn

Legend:
- Tropical moist forest (evergreen and seasonal)
- Boreal forest
- Temperate forest (mixed)
- Temperate forest (broadleaf)
- Dry woodland
- Mountain
- Non-forest land

Robinson Projection

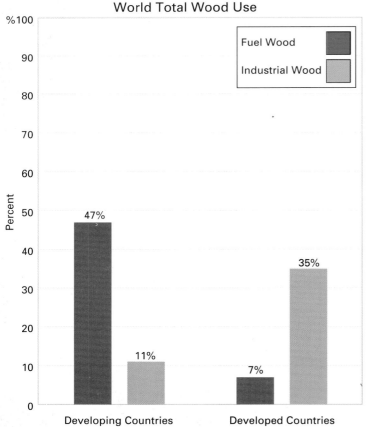

World Total Wood Use

%100

- Fuel Wood
- Industrial Wood

Percent

47%
11%
7%
35%

Developing Countries   Developed Countries

Reforestation projects like this one help maintain the world's forests.

QUICK FACTS
Of the earth's total land area, 6% is rainforest. Rainforests contain almost 90% of the world's plant and animal species.

Annual world wood consumption is 3 billion m³ (118 billion cu. ft.). Forests are the source of fuel for 50% of the world's population.

27

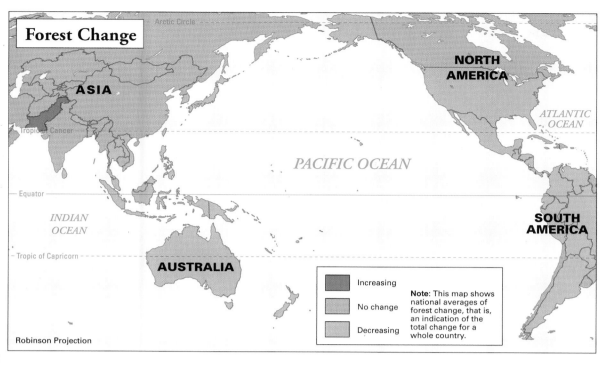

Forest Change

Note: This map shows national averages of forest change, that is, an indication of the total change for a whole country.

Legend:
- Increasing
- No change
- Decreasing

Robinson Projection

ASIA · NORTH AMERICA · ATLANTIC OCEAN · PACIFIC OCEAN · SOUTH AMERICA · INDIAN OCEAN · AUSTRALIA

Arctic Circle · Tropic of Cancer · Equator · Tropic of Capricorn

Forest Cover in Selected Countries

Country	Percent
Japan	66.5 %
Bhutan	54.4 %
Canada	36.1 %
USA	30.6 %
China	12.6 %
Singapore	5.0 %

Boreal Forest · Temperate Forest · Tropical Forest

There are three general types of forests.

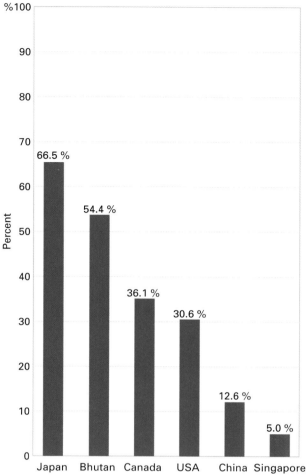

Forests like this one in Japan are beautiful to look at and to visit.

Forest Cover Changes in Selected Countries (1976-91)

Thousands of Hectares

Canada	+27 700 Th
Japan	+94 Th
Philippines	−3 120 Th
Malaysia	−3 220 Th
Thailand	−3 960 Th
USA	−12 200 Th
Indonesia	−12 600 Th
Chin	−13 509 Th

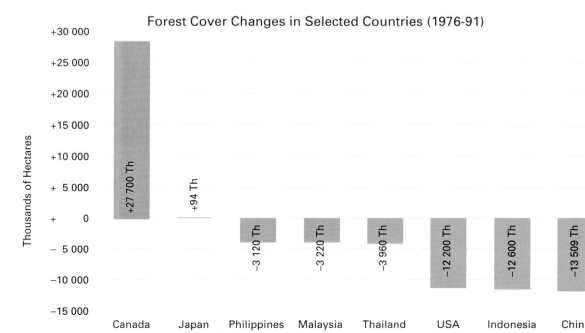

Rubber is a harvested forest product in Malaysia.

Energy Uses and Resources

Energy use tells us a great deal about a society or country. Generally speaking, the more industrialized a country is, the more energy it uses. Industrialized countries tend to use a great deal of electricity. Electricity can be produced from hydro power, nuclear power plants, or generators driven by fossil fuels.

As well, fossil fuels — coal, oil, and natural gas — are also used by industrial nations to power transportation, steel production, home heating, and other activities.

Some Pacific Rim countries have more resources than others. Brunei, Indonesia, and Canada, for example, have so many energy resources that they can export them to other countries. Japan, Hong Kong, and Singapore, on the other hand, are almost completely dependent on imported sources of energy. This makes trade in energy resources an important economic activity.

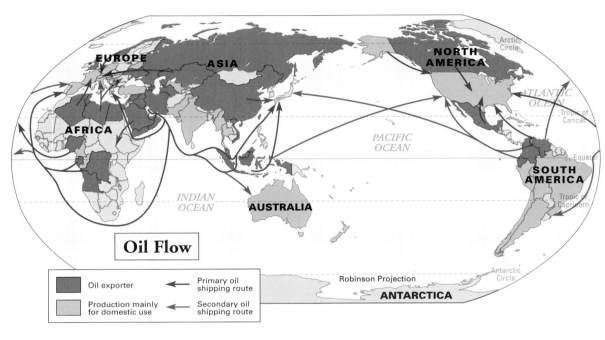

Oil Flow

Oil exporter — ← Primary oil shipping route
Production mainly for domestic use — ← Secondary oil shipping route

Robinson Projection

Energy Exports and Imports for Selected Countries

(Million Tonnes of Coal-Equivalent)

Imports / Exports

Canada: 62 M, 151 M
China: 7.7 M, 61 M
Indonesia: 13 M, 112 M
Japan: 507 M, 11 M
South Korea: 102 M, 4.8 M
USA: 588 M, 131 M

Canada produces approximately 64.5 million tonnes (63.5 million tons) of coal each year. Much of it is exported from facilities similar to the Neptune Terminal in Vancouver, British Columbia.

Hydroelectric plants are one source of electricity in Japan.

Energy Reserves of Selected Countries

Country	Uranium (Thousands of Tonnes)	Coal (Millions of Tonnes)	Natural Gas (Billions of Cubic Meters)	Crude Petroleum (Millions of Barrels)
Canada	146	6 966	2 739	5 586
China	51	730 700	1 002	24 000
Indonesia	4	3 000	2 952	11 846
Japan	0	873	33	60
South Korea	0	158	0	0
USA	102	215 241	4 794	26 250

QUICK FACTS
Of all the energy produced in the world: the United States uses 30%; India uses 2%
China produces more coal than any other country in the world.

29

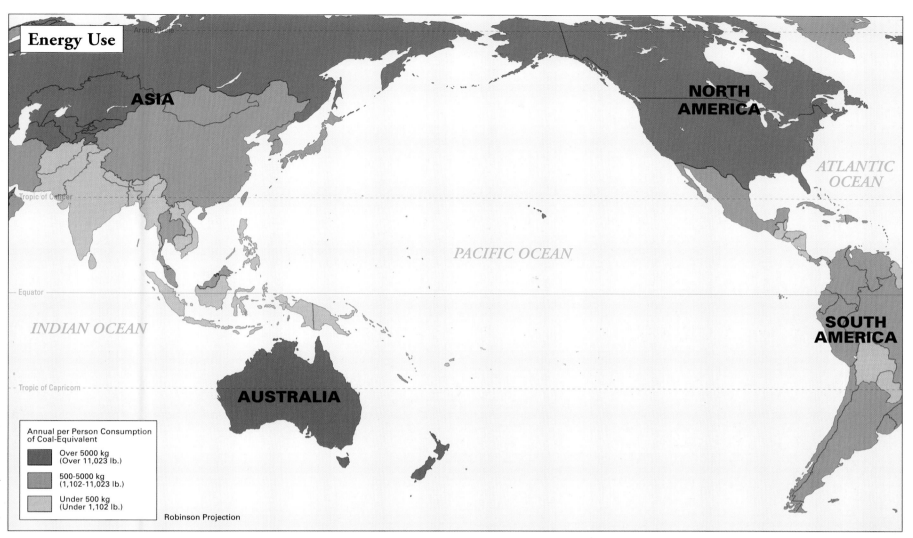

Energy Use

Annual per Person Consumption
of Coal-Equivalent

Over 5000 kg
(Over 11,023 lb.)

500-5000 kg
(1,102-11,023 lb.)

Under 500 kg
(Under 1,102 lb.)

Robinson Projection

Energy Consumption per Person per Year in Selected Countries

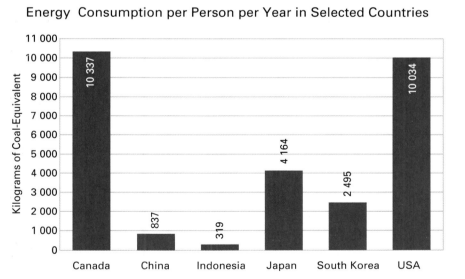

Kilograms of Coal-Equivalent

Canada	China	Indonesia	Japan	South Korea	USA
10 337	837	319	4 164	2 495	10 034

World Oil Demand

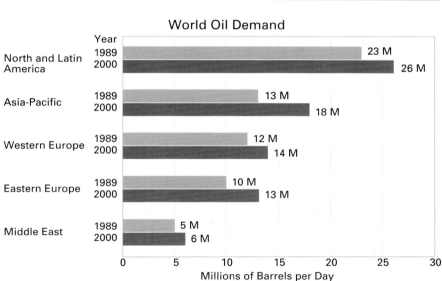

	Year		
North and Latin America	1989	23 M	
	2000	26 M	
Asia-Pacific	1989	13 M	
	2000	18 M	
Western Europe	1989	12 M	
	2000	14 M	
Eastern Europe	1989	10 M	
	2000	13 M	
Middle East	1989	5 M	
	2000	6 M	

Millions of Barrels per Day

In many countries, dung is an important source of fuel to heat homes and cook food; this is an environmentally friendly method.

Geothermal plants are used to make electricity from the natural heat produced from the earth. They are an environmentally friendly way of creating power, because they cause little pollution.

Endangered Earth

Every country in the world has environmental problems of some kind. The growth of cities, towns, factories, and farms over time has created many benefits for humanity. But, it has also changed the balance of the earth's natural systems in ways never intended. Fortunately, we are becoming more aware of the problems and making attempts to solve them through conservation, recycling, and other means.

The environmental issues in the Pacific Rim are no different from those in the rest of the world. Some problems are less serious than others, affecting only local conditions. Others might have an impact that is felt around the globe.

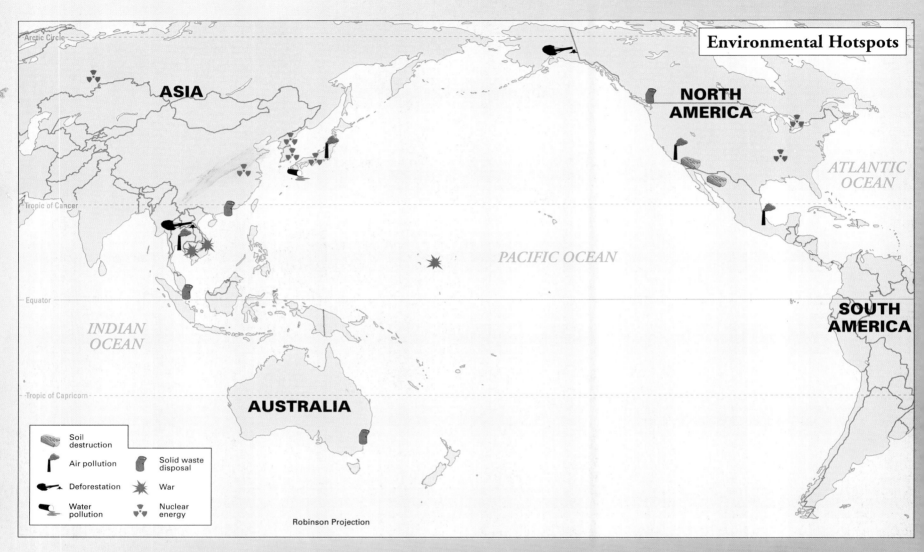

Environmental Hotspots

ASIA

NORTH AMERICA

ATLANTIC OCEAN

PACIFIC OCEAN

SOUTH AMERICA

INDIAN OCEAN

AUSTRALIA

Arctic Circle

Tropic of Cancer

Equator

Tropic of Capricorn

Soil destruction

Air pollution

Deforestation

Water pollution

Solid waste disposal

War

Nuclear energy

Robinson Projection

Soil Destruction

Farming is the major method of food production. Soil, therefore, is an important natural resource that must be carefully managed. Land is sometimes overused by being planted too often or allowing animals to graze too long. Chemicals like pesticides can cause serious damage to the soil. Erosion by wind and water means soil simply disappears, consumed by natural forces.

In some areas, farmers need to use water from rivers and lakes to irrigate their fields. This can lead to serious problems as the sun's heat causes the water to evaporate, carrying mineral salts to the soil surface. The crops being grown in salt-contaminated fields often die. The hot, dry regions of Mexico and southern California experience this problem, called salinization.

Air Pollution

The main cause of air pollution is the burning of fossil fuels. Many countries use coal, petroleum, and natural gas to provide power for industry and for transportation systems. When these fuels are burned, they produce by-products such as soot, carbon monoxide, and carbon dioxide. The result is the smog that is found in all large cities, particularly major centers like Los Angeles, Mexico City, Tokyo, and Bangkok.

The air pollution from fossil fuels also contributes to acid rain. Not only does acid rain contaminate drinking water, it injures plant and marine life, as well as damaging buildings and metal structures.

QUICK FACTS Every North American creates approximately one tonne (2205 lb.) of garbage per year.
Total number of nuclear reactors in the Pacific Rim region: 200
Asia "loses" an estimated 25 billion tonnes (24.6 billion tons) of soil each year.

31

Water Pollution

Water is essential to all forms of life on earth. When the water supply becomes polluted, human, animal, and marine life are all endangered. Industrial wastes and human sewage sometimes enter rivers and lakes, resulting in poisoned fish, and contaminated water. When humans drink the water or eat the fish, the results can be disastrous.

One example of the effects of water pollution is Minamata Disease, named for the Japanese town where it was first identified. At one time, local industries were getting rid of their wastes by dumping them into the nearby river and the ocean. One of the substances disposed of in this way was mercury, a heavy metal. After several years of eating fish that had been caught in local waters, some residents of Minamata fell ill, poisoned by the mercury in the fish. The results of mercury poisoning, or Minamata Disease, can be severe, with permanent brain damage and injury to the nervous system.

Nuclear Energy

There are approximately 200 nuclear reactors in the countries of the Pacific Rim. Japan, Russia, China, Korea, Canada, and the United States all use nuclear reactors to generate some of their electricity supplies.

Nuclear technology has not yet developed reactors that are totally safe, nor a secure method for disposing of nuclear wastes. So, while nuclear energy is potentially one of the most useful energy sources, it still can cause serious environmental problems. The most widely known nuclear accident in recent years was at Chernobyl, Russia, in 1986, when the reactors' cooling system failed and the core overheated, resulting in fire. The radioactive fall-out from this incident was widespread.

Solid Waste Disposal

As cities and towns grow, so does the amount of waste material their residents create. Consumer goods are sold in packages that are made of paper, plastic, or cardboard. Manufactured products, from automobiles to clothes, eventually wear out or break down and have to be disposed of when they are replaced. Newspapers, books, and magazines have a limited useful life before they too are consigned to the garbage. Tonnes of hospital wastes and industrial by-products accumulate daily, waiting for disposal.

Landfill sites, where garbage is buried, eventually become full. Often, there is no new land available for the next dump to be created. Some cities ship their waste out to sea in barges, dumping it in open water. But this can create even more environmental problems, when the garbage is washed ashore to pollute

coastlines and beaches. A few towns and cities incinerate their garbage, burning it at very high temperatures and using the heat to generate electricity. However, many people believe that disposing of waste in this way adds to air pollution.

War

War damages the economy as well as the environment. The chemicals and weapons used destroy forests, contaminate the soil, and disrupt drainage and irrigation systems in fields. The effects of the Vietnam War (1954-1975) are still being felt in that nation. Similarly, the lengthy civil war in Cambodia has left a lasting impact on the country's natural systems.

The testing of military weapons can also damage the environment. The Pacific atoll of Bikini, for example, was used by the United

States between 1946 and 1958 for the testing of nuclear bombs. All the local residents were evacuated in 1946. In 1969, they were allowed to return, only to be re-evacuated in 1978 when tests showed that radiation levels on the atoll were still very high. Clean-up efforts began in 1988.

Deforestation

Forests are renewable resources that will grow back over time if they are allowed to do so. Many times, though, trees are cut and not replaced. At other times new trees are planted, but not before serious soil damage — that affects how well they will grow — has occurred.

The forests are disappearing from many areas of the Pacific Rim. Timber is needed to build houses and make furniture. Trees must be felled to clear land for farming, and to use as fuel for cooking and heating. From Alaska to the tropical jungles of Southeast Asia, trees are being used faster than they are being replaced. In 1950, for example, 53% of Thailand's total land area was forest-covered. By 1991, that figure had shrunk to only 27%. Elsewhere, the story is the same, though many countries are now making an effort to conserve their forests.

Measures of Well-Being

Living standards can be measured in many different ways. Comparative wealth, life expectancy, nutrition, and infant mortality are four of the categories often used to do so.

A country's GDP, or Gross Domestic Product, indicates the wealth within the country. To calculate the GDP, economists add up the value of all the goods and services produced entirely within the country. (Gross National Product, or GNP, includes income the country has received from foreign sources.)

One of the best measures of living standards is nutrition. A country in which the people have enought to eat is considered to have a good standard of living.

A country's life expectancy is the average number of years its citizens can expect to live.

In Canada, for example, life expectancy is 74 years for men, and 81 years for women.

The infant mortality rate is the number of children per 1000 live births who die before reaching the age of one year. A low infant mortality rate indicates that health-care standards are high in that country.

Nutrition

According to the United Nations, a person needs at least 2500 calories daily to stay healthy. The nutritional value of these calories must be considered, though; a diet with a balance between carbohydrates, proteins, and fats is best. A balanced diet provides all the vitamins, minerals, and calories people need to work and maintain healthy bodies.

Many people meet their daily caloric needs with food high in carbohydrates. What their diet often lacks is food high in proteins. Such people may face malnutrition caused by protein deficiency. Malnourished people are more vulnerable to diseases and may die at an earlier age. For others, the food problem is overeating; this is especially true of food high in fats. Fast foods, such as hamburgers and fried potatoes, are high-fat foods. A diet high in fat can lead to circulatory problems that may eventually cause heart attacks and strokes.

Male/Female Literacy Rates for Selected Countries

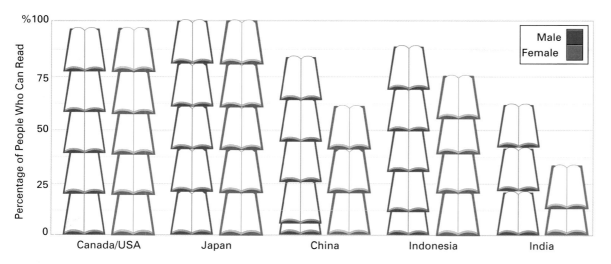

An adult literacy class in the Philippines helps students learn to read and write.

GDP per Person for Selected Countries

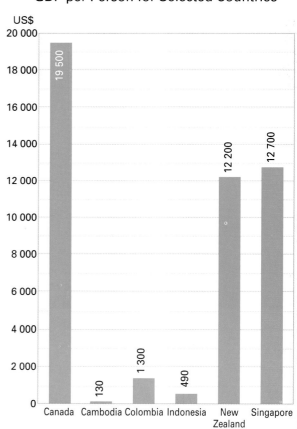

A country's GDP, or Gross Domestic Product, indicates the value of all the goods and services produced within the country in a year. The GDP per person is figured out by dividing the GDP by the total number of people in the country. GDP per person can be misleading as a measure of living standards. For example, a country could have a high GDP per person. The wealth, though, could be in the hands of very few people. Thus, many people in that country would be poor.

QUICK FACTS
Pacific Rim country with:
- the most physicians: China (1 763 000)
- the highest doctor/patient ratio: New Zealand (1:359)
- the lowest doctor/patient ratio: Cambodia (1:27 000)

33

At this health clinic in the Philippines, children receive expert medical care.

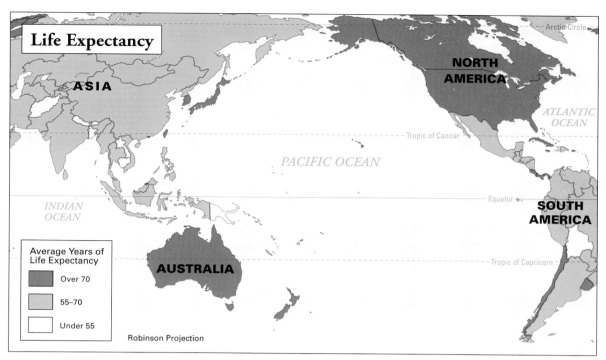

Life Expectancy

Average Years of Life Expectancy

- Over 70
- 55–70
- Under 55

Robinson Projection

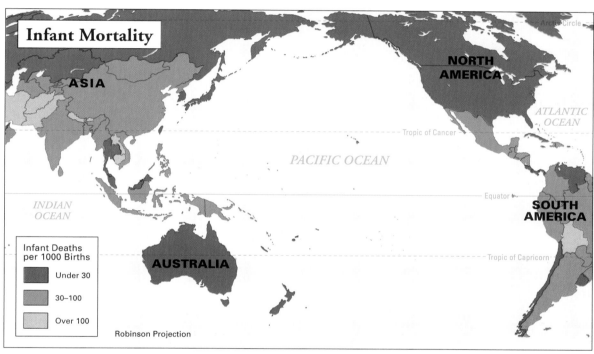

Infant Mortality

Infant Deaths per 1000 Births

- Under 30
- 30–100
- Over 100

Robinson Projection

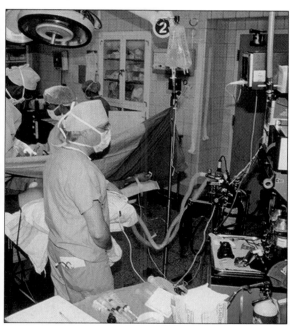

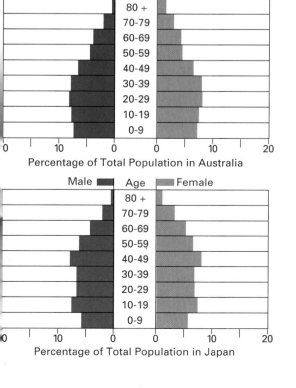

The high standard of living in Canada can be measured by the number of well-equipped hospitals, such as this one in Toronto.

Population Pyramids for Selected Countries

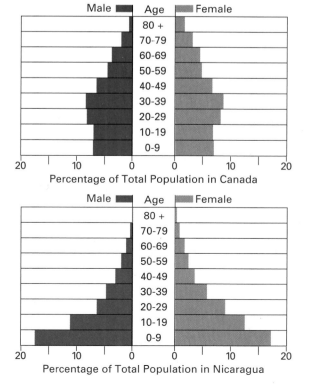

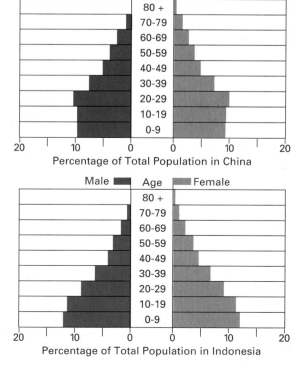

Percentage of Total Population in Australia

Percentage of Total Population in Canada

Percentage of Total Population in China

Percentage of Total Population in Japan

Percentage of Total Population in Nicaragua

Percentage of Total Population in Indonesia

Gateways to the Pacific

The Pacific Ocean is the main unifying feature of the nations of the Pacific Rim. Many of the world's largest, busiest seaports are located here. They handle millions of tonnes of raw materials and finished products destined for local and international trade.

Much of the economic growth of Pacific Rim countries is based on shipping and trading activities.

Modern port cities, such as Tokyo, Singapore, Sydney, Auckland, Vancouver, and Seattle, have a variety of docks and ship-handling facilities. Each port is able to deal with many different types of ships and cargoes. Container ships, roll-on/roll-off carriers, bulk carriers, and freighters all pass through the ports of the Pacific Rim.

Tokyo, Japan

Singapore

Sydney, Australia

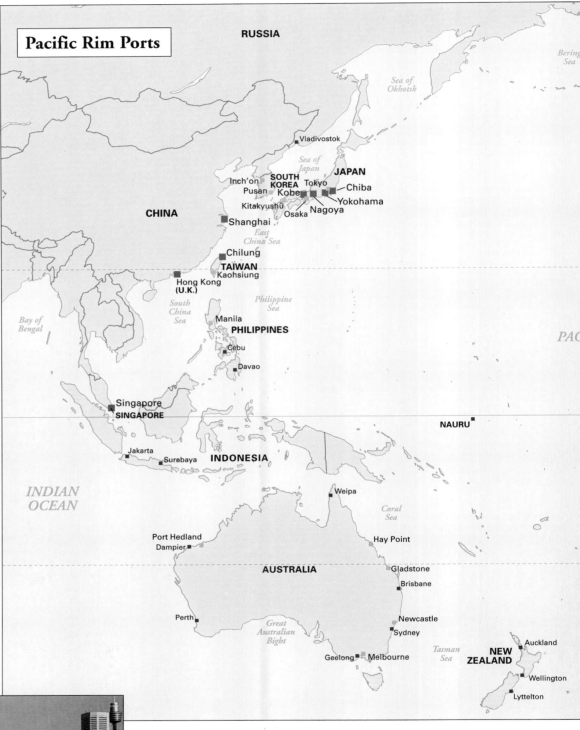

Pacific Rim Ports

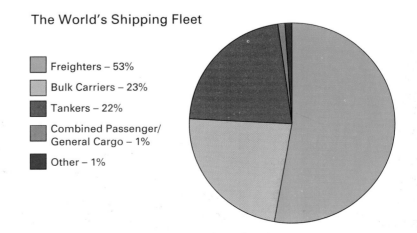

The World's Shipping Fleet

- Freighters – 53%
- Bulk Carriers – 23%
- Tankers – 22%
- Combined Passenger/ General Cargo – 1%
- Other – 1%

QUICK FACTS
Hong Kong is the world's busiest container port.   Japan owns 6% of the world's merchant fleet.
There are more than 80 000 merchant vessels in the world's fleet.

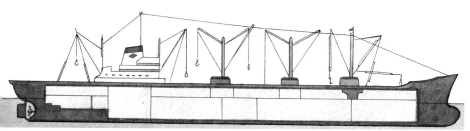

Ordinary freighters make good use of all available space for cargo.

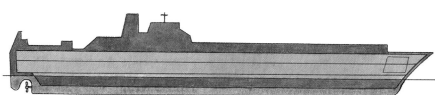

Cars are simply driven on and off roll-on/roll-off ("ro-ro") carriers like this one.

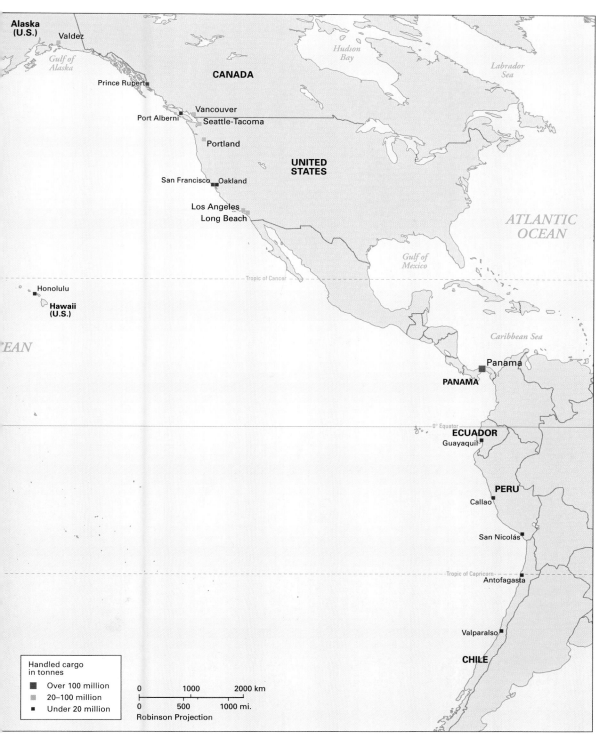

Handled cargo in tonnes
■ Over 100 million
■ 20–100 million
■ Under 20 million

0   1000   2000 km
0   500   1000 mi.
Robinson Projection

Major Seaports of the Region

Port	Thousands of Tonnes Handled
Singapore	206 429 Th
Kobe, Japan	174 101 Th
Shanghai, China	139 590 Th
Nagoya, Japan	136 794 Th
Yokohama, Japan	121 942 Th
Hong Kong	104 502 Th
Kitakyushu, Japan	98 680 Th
Osaka, Japan	98 659 Th
Tokyo, Japan	79 335 Th
Kaohsiung, Taiwan	77 126 Th
Inch'on, South Korea	70 959 Th
Los Angeles, USA	70 910 Th
Vancouver, Canada	70 714 Th
Seattle, USA	19 864 Th
Sydney, Australia	19 588 Th

Thousands of Tonnes Handled

Auckland, New Zealand

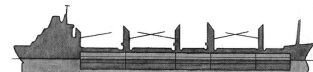

Bulk carriers are used for transporting raw materials such as coal, potash, grain, and iron ore.

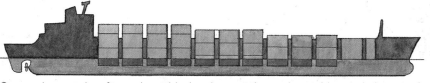

General cargo is often placed in large containers (metal boxes) that are then moved directly onto trucks or rail cars from the ship.

Trade: The Lifeblood of the Region

Trade has long been the single most important factor linking the countries of the Pacific Rim. For centuries, caravans traveled along the famous Silk Road. Chinese and Arab traders sailed through the waters of South and Southeast Asia carrying goods from as far away as Africa and India to lands on the edge of the Pacific.

Today, several of the world's leading trading nations, including Japan, the United States, and Canada, are members of the Pacific Rim community of nations. Some of the newly developed countries, such as Hong Kong and Singapore, depend on trade to a very large extent for their high standard of living. Even the less developed countries, such as Vietnam, are now trying to become more important trading nations in order to improve the standard of living of their people.

The Pacific Rim is the fastest-growing economic region of the world.

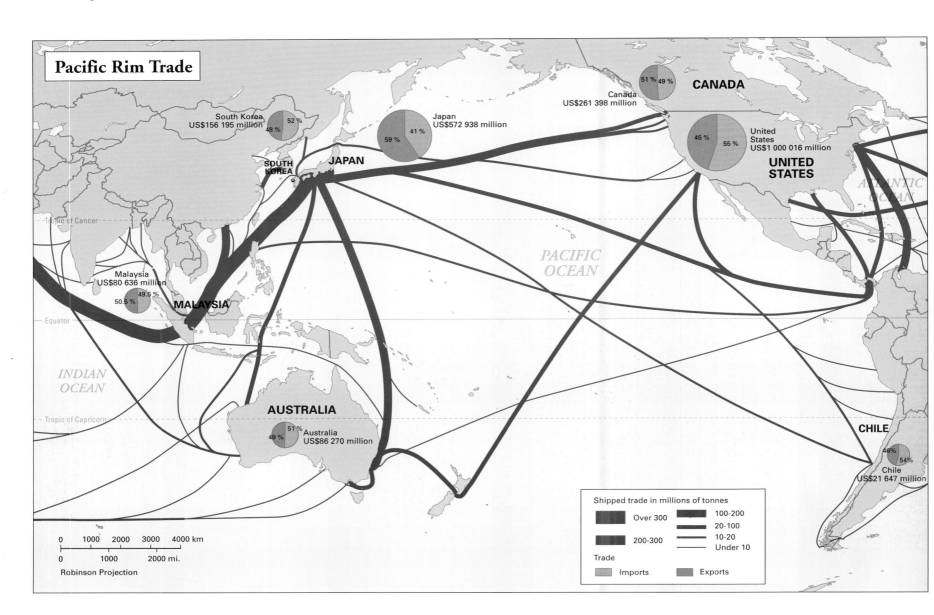

Pacific Rim Trade

South Korea
US$156 195 million
48% / 52%

Japan
US$572 938 million
59% / 41%

Canada
US$261 398 million
51% / 49%
CANADA

United States
US$1 000 016 million
45% / 55%
UNITED STATES

SOUTH KOREA   JAPAN

Malaysia
US$80 636 million
50.5% / 49.5%
MALAYSIA

PACIFIC OCEAN

INDIAN OCEAN

ATLANTIC OCEAN

Tropic of Cancer

Equator

Tropic of Capricorn

AUSTRALIA
51% / 49%
Australia
US$86 270 million

CHILE
46% / 54%
Chile
US$21 647 million

0 1000 2000 3000 4000 km
0 1000 2000 mi.
Robinson Projection

Shipped trade in millions of tonnes
Over 300   100-200
200-300   20-100
                10-20
                Under 10
Trade
Imports
Exports

Coffee from Guatemala, kiwi fruit from New Zealand, and newsprint from Australia are some of the many import and export products of the Pacific Rim.

QUICK FACTS
Diamonds and oil are major exports for Indonesia.
China is the largest consumer market in the world.

Of Japan's total imports, 40% comes from other countries in Asia.

Imports and Exports – Selected Pacific Rim Countries

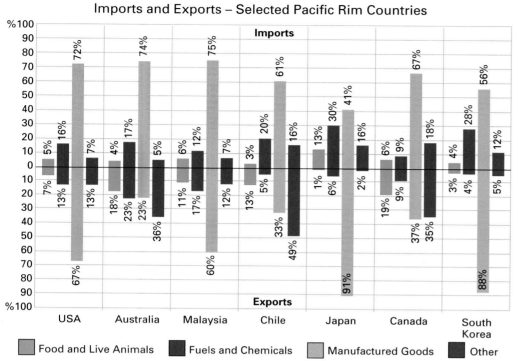

Legend:
- Food and Live Animals
- Fuels and Chemicals
- Manufactured Goods
- Other

Trade Growth, 1986-1992 Selected Pacific Rim Countries

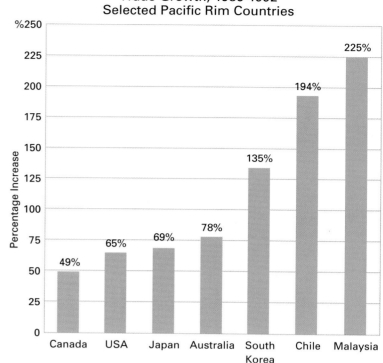

Cars are produced in many Pacific Rim countries. They are built in modern factories and shipped around the world. Here, cars imported from Japan wait for delivery at a Vancouver dock.

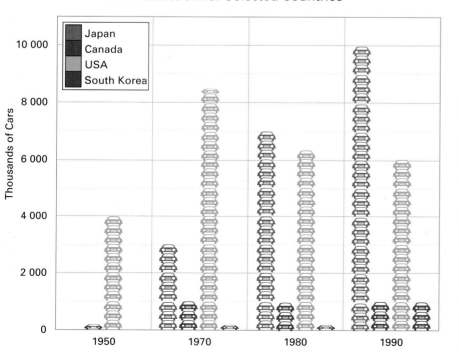

Percentage of Trade in the Pacific Rim for Selected Countries

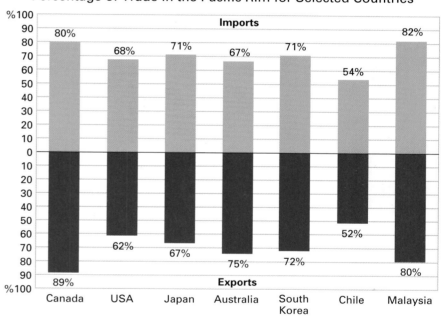

Car Production for Selected Countries

Legend:
- Japan
- Canada
- USA
- South Korea

Major Trading Blocs

	Total GDP	GDP per Person	Population
European Community: Belgium, Denmark, France, Germany, Greece, Ireland, Italy, Luxembourg, Netherlands, Portugal, Spain, United Kingdom	US$6.4 trillion	US$17 584	344 800 000
North American Free Trade Agreement: Canada, USA, Mexico	US$7 trillion	US$16 971	366 900 000
Asian Free Trade Agreement: Brunei, Indonesia, Malaysia, Philippines, Singapore, Thailand	US$359 billion	US$4 464	331 470 000

The Riches of the "Indies"

Today, goods and people travel from one country of the Pacific Rim to another by airplane, steamship, railway, or road. For many centuries, however, cargoes and passengers moved much more slowly within this vast region. Overland, they moved on the backs of camels or horses along routes such as the famed "Silk Road". Wooden sailing ships — Arab dhows and Chinese junks — carried cargoes through the fabled waters of the Indian Ocean, the Strait of Malacca, and the South China Sea.

European trade with the Pacific Rim region began in Roman times. It was in the 16th century, however, that European trade with both sides of the Pacific developed. European navigators sailed westward across the Atlantic and south around Africa in search of water routes to the riches of the "Indies".

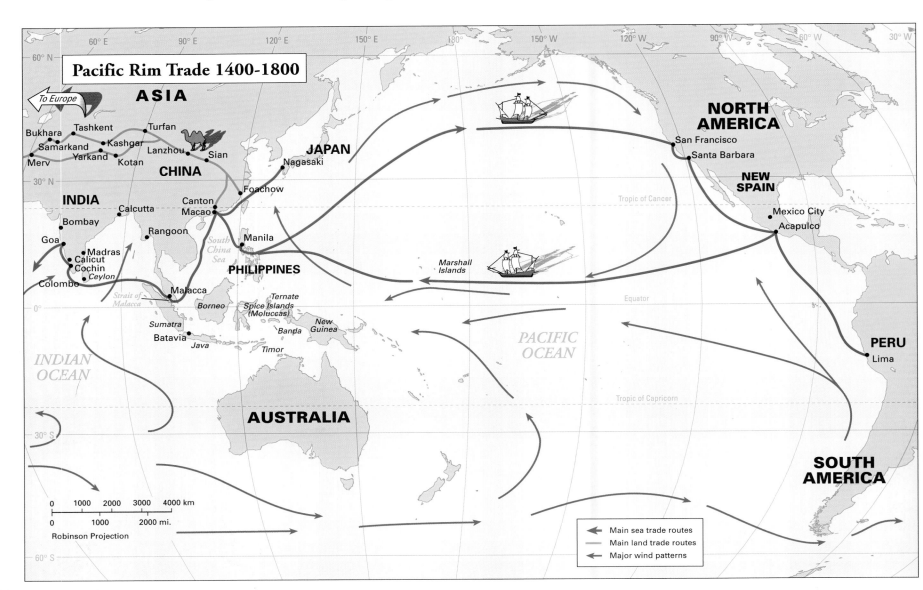

Pacific Rim Trade 1400-1800

→	Main sea trade routes
—	Main land trade routes
→	Major wind patterns

Caravans might consist of 400 camels and stretch about 1.5 km (0.9 mi.). Each camel could carry 270 kg (595 lb.) of merchandise.

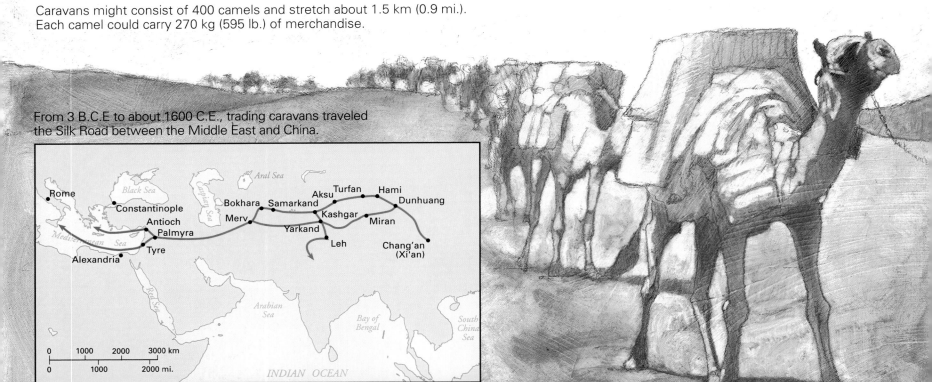

From 3 B.C.E to about 1600 C.E., trading caravans traveled the Silk Road between the Middle East and China.

QUICK FACTS
In 1392, China planted 50 million trees to be used in shipbuilding.   In 1077 B.C.E., China produced 20 million bales of silk.
Five-masted Chinese junks carried over 1000 crew members.   Spices from Asia sold in Europe for over 300 times their cost.

39

From the Americas

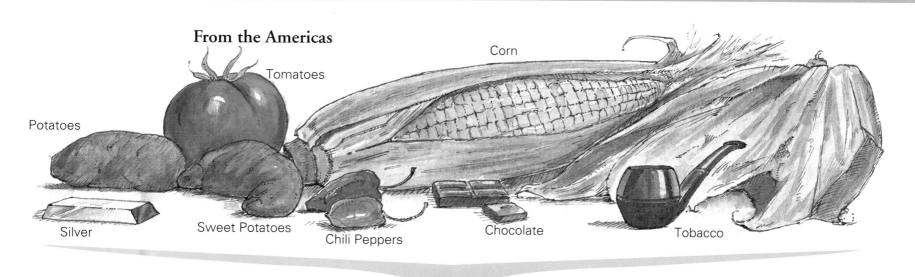

Potatoes

Tomatoes

Corn

Silver

Sweet Potatoes

Chili Peppers

Chocolate

Tobacco

Tea

Oils and Fragrances

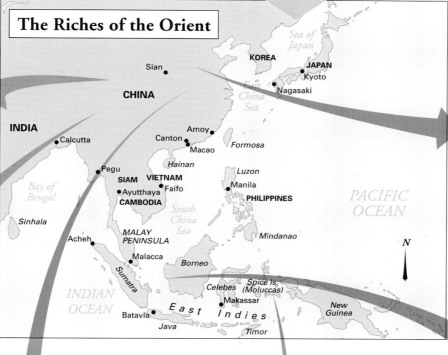

The Riches of the Orient

Sian

KOREA   JAPAN
Kyoto

CHINA

Nagasaki

Sea of Japan

East China Sea

INDIA

Calcutta

Amoy

Canton

Macao

Formosa

Hainan

Pegu

Luzon

SIAM   VIETNAM

Faifo

Manila

Ayutthaya

CAMBODIA

PHILIPPINES

PACIFIC OCEAN

Bay of Bengal

South China Sea

Sinhala

Acheh

MALAY PENINSULA

Mindanao

Malacca

Borneo

N

Sumatra

Celebes

Spice Is. (Moluccas)

INDIAN OCEAN

Batavia

East Indies

Makassar

New Guinea

Java

Timor

Porcelain

Art Treasures

Silk

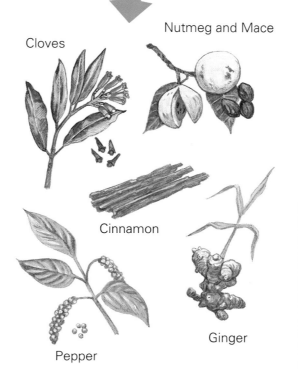

Cloves

Nutmeg and Mace

Cinnamon

Pepper

Ginger

Approximate Cost of Goods for an Ordinary Worker in 1200 C.E.	
to buy	**cost**
1m (1.09 yd.) of silk =	22 days' wages
10 g (0.4 oz.) of pepper =	6 days' wages
10 g (0.4 oz.) of cinnamon =	1½ days' wages
10 g (0.4 oz.) of ginger =	4 days' wages

Into the Unknown

Thanks to science, the first space explorers journeyed beyond earth with some knowledge of what to expect. This was not true of most early travelers and explorers. They had no maps to follow, only crude navigational instruments to guide them, and no firm knowledge of other lands. Traveling conditions, on both land and sea, were harsh and filled with danger. Years might pass without travelers having any contact with their homelands. In spite of these hardships, many were spurred on by their desire for gold, glory, and knowledge, or by religious fervor. These early explorers were among the map makers and scientists of their day.

Travelers, explorers, and traders came from China, Africa, North America, and Europe to Southeast Asia. There were many thriving cultures in this region long before these explorers arrived.

Each year, Manila galleons, loaded with silver from the mines of New Spain, set sail from Acapulco headed for Manila.

By the end of the 14th century, **Ibn Battuta** (1304-1369), King of Travelers, had visited more of the known world than any person before him. Starting from Tangiers, he journeyed through 44 countries in Africa, Asia, Russia, Southeast Asia, and China.

In the early 15th century, **Zheng He** (1371-1435) set out from China to explore Southeast Asia, India, and Africa. He made a total of seven expeditions.

The five-masted junks of admiral Zheng He were many times larger than the ships of European explorers.

Ferdinand Magellan (1480-1521) is honored as the first person to sail around the globe, even though he himself never completed the journey. He died one month after crossing the Pacific Ocean.

First Around the World
- set sail on September 19, 1519
- journey started from Spain with five ships
- 237 members in the crews
- whole trip took three years
- only one ship, the *Vittoria*, returned
- 18 crew members survived
- took 98 days to sail the 20 800 km (13,000 mi.) across the Pacific

Captain James Cook (1728-1779) was a great navigator who, during three voyages, traveled to New Zealand, Australia, and many of the Pacific islands. He visited Hawaii and the west coast of North America. Unlike many other sea captains at the time, Cook was very popular with his crew.

QUICK FACTS
Sailing time across the Pacific in 1519: 98 days   Chinese invented first compass: 1000 C.E.

41

Routes of Exploration: 1271–1780 C.E.

Legend:
- Marco Polo, 1271-95
- Ibn Battuta, 1330-49
- Zheng He, 1431-33
- Magellan, 1519-22
- Portuguese trade route, 1500-1600
- Spanish galleon trade, 1565-1815
- Drake, 1577-80
- Cook, 1776-80

Robinson Projection

Scale: 0 1000 2000 3000 4000 km / 0 1000 2000 mi.

Sir Francis Drake (1543-1596) also sailed around the world. His voyage lasted three years, from 1577 to 1580.

Drake's ship, the *Golden Hind,* was only 30 m (98.5 ft.) long. It weighed just under 91 tonnes (89.5 tons). Yet, in this vessel, Drake sailed around the world. A modern cruise ship can weigh as much as 227 000 tonnes (223,000 tons). The *Golden Hind* looks like a toy in comparison.

Religions of the East

Religion plays an important part in many Asian societies. Most of the world's major religions, Hinduism, Buddhism, Christianity, Shintoism, Judaism, and Islam, are represented in Asia.

Religion is part of everyday life for many Asian people. It affects the way they do business, design their buildings, and prepare their food.

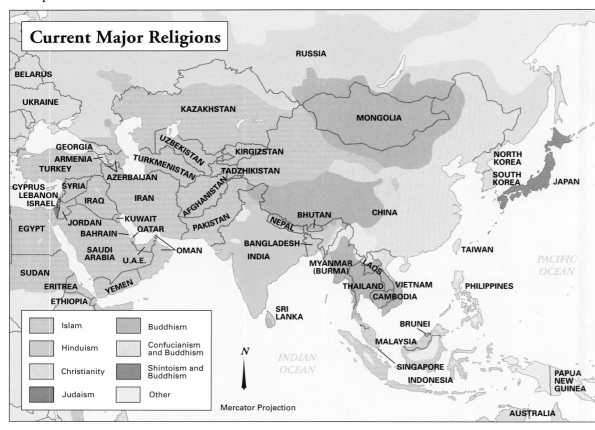

Current Major Religions

Legend:
- Islam
- Hinduism
- Christianity
- Judaism
- Buddhism
- Confucianism and Buddhism
- Shintoism and Buddhism
- Other

Mercator Projection

Buddhism began in India in the 6th century B.C.E. This statue of Buddha is in the compound of the Phra That Doi Suthep temple, at Chiang Mai, northern Thailand.

Religions in Selected Countries

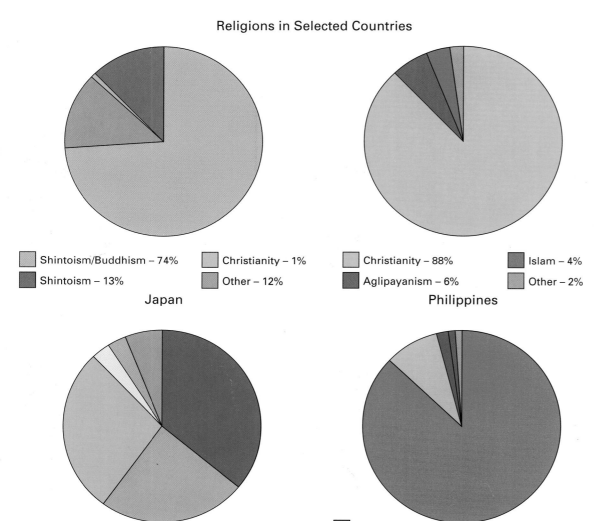

Japan
- Shintoism/Buddhism – 74%
- Shintoism – 13%
- Christianity – 1%
- Other – 12%

Philippines
- Christianity – 88%
- Aglipayanism – 6%
- Islam – 4%
- Other – 2%

South Korea
- Buddhism – 36%
- Confucianism – 24%
- Christianity – 28%
- Wonbulgyo – 3%
- Chondogyo – 3%
- Other – 6%

Indonesia
- Islam – 87%
- Christianity – 9%
- Hinduism – 2%
- Buddhism – 1%
- Other – 1%

Thailand
- Buddhism – 94%
- Islam – 4%
- Christianity – 0.5%
- Other – 1.5%

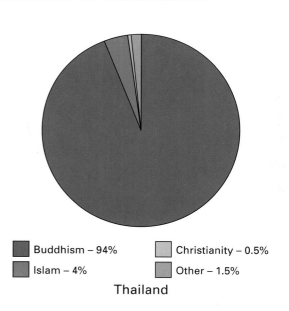

This Thai wedding ceremony is being celebrated in the Buddhist tradition.

QUICK FACTS
Hinduism was founded in India, around 1500 B.C.E.
Buddhism was founded in India, around 525 B.C.E.

Christianity was founded in Palestine, in the 1st century C.E.
Islam was founded in Medina, Arabia, around 622 C.E.

43

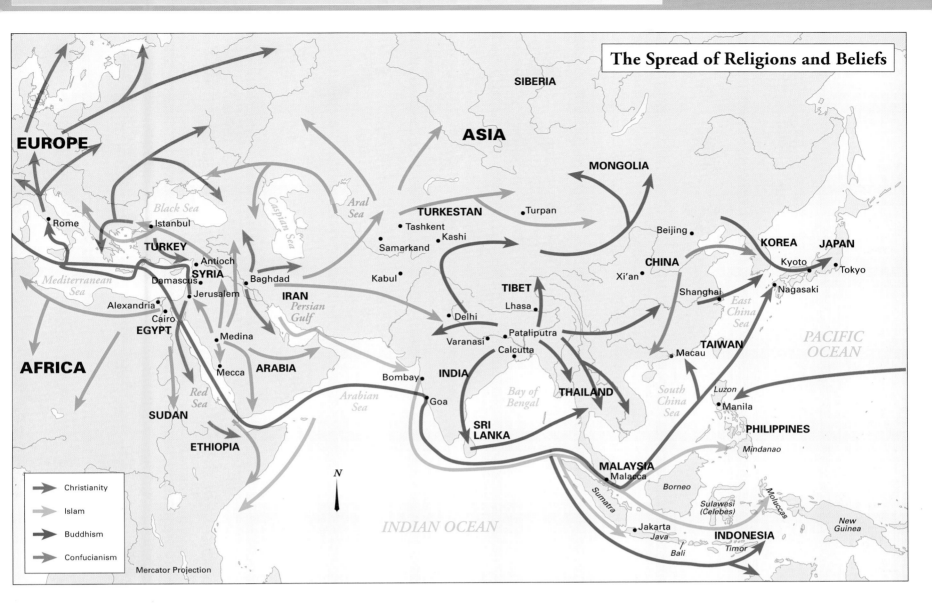

The Spread of Religions and Beliefs

Legend:
- Christianity
- Islam
- Buddhism
- Confucianism

Mercator Projection

Islam is a dominant religion in Southeast Asia. This Muslim boy is attending a service with his father.

This is a Hindu cremation ceremony in Bali.

The Shinto festival of Sanja is being celebrated here at a shrine in Tokyo.

Pagodas are a distinctive feature of Buddhist architecture. This one is in Hong Kong.

Although Buddhism began in India, there are very few Buddhists in that nation today.

This Christian church at Penang, Malaysia, was built in the early 19th century.

Singapore is a cosmopolitan country. Many of the religions of Asia are found here, including Hinduism.

A Land of Contrasts

In India, ancient customs and traditions exist side by side with the latest advances in science and technology.

The Himalayas, the world's highest mountain range, form the northern boundary of the nation. South of the mountains, the major river systems provide fertile valleys that have attracted the largest portion of the country's population. Agriculture and abundant natural resources, like forests, fossil fuels, and minerals, form the basis of India's economy.

Projected at more than 900 million in 1994, India's population is in size second only to China's. Such a large population includes many ethnic groups, each having its own language and religion. In modern India, Hinduism is the religion of the majority, and Hindi is an official language. English is also used widely in government and education, and the constitution recognizes fourteen other languages.

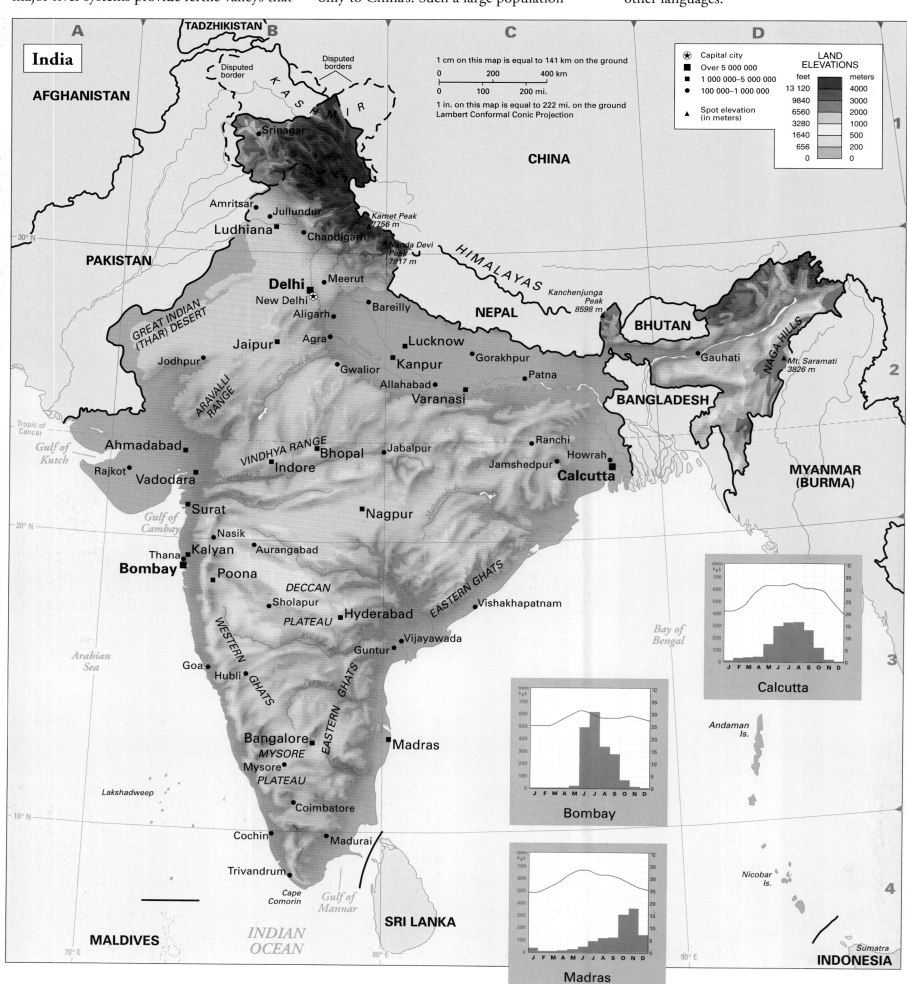

QUICK FACTS
Area: 3 287 590 km² (1,269,010 sq. mi.)
Population (1994): 911 576 000

Imports (1992): US$23 638 million
Exports (1992): US$20 683 million

45

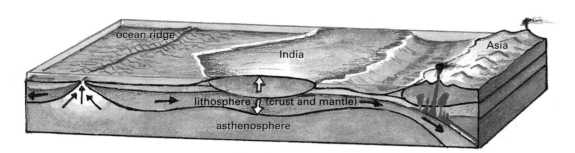

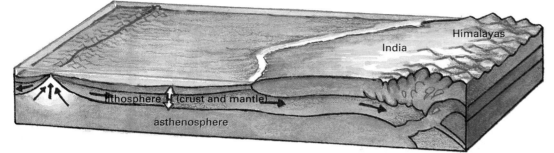

The Himalaya Mountains form the northern boundary of India and Nepal. The Ganges Plain, at the foot of the mountains, is fertile, well-watered, and densely populated.

The collision of the Indian and Eurasian Plates about 45 million years ago produced the majestic Himalayas.

New Delhi is a city of broad streets, historic monuments, such as the India Gate shown here, and magnificent government buildings.

Major Languages in India

- Hindi – 37.9%
- Other – 9.9%
- Telugu – 7.8%
- Bengali – 7.4%
- Marathi – 7.1%
- Tamil – 6.4%
- Urdu – 5.1%
- Gujarati – 4.8%
- Kannada – 3.9%
- Malayalan – 3.7%
- Oriya – 3.3%
- Punjabi – 2.7%

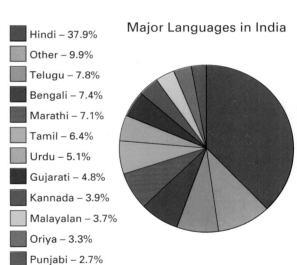

This region, near India's southwest coast, receives heavy rain. The rivers, flowing fully, are important local transportation routes.

Calcutta is home to more than twelve million people. The city is a major center of industry, trade, and commerce.

The Ganges River in northern India is considered sacred by Hindus. There are many shrines and places of pilgrimage along its banks. The river also provides a major source of water for irrigation.

One of Our Oldest Civilizations

India's history can be traced to 3000 B.C.E., to the people living in the valley of the Indus River. Around 1500 B.C.E., Aryans from southwest Asia gradually blended their culture with that of the earlier inhabitants. Their combined religious beliefs became Hinduism, whose sacred texts were written between 1200 and 100 B.C.E. During this time, another of the world's great religions began in India with Siddhartha Gautama Buddha, born in the 6th century B.C.E.

For centuries, India's many ethnic groups lived as separate kingdoms or states, each with its own leader, language or dialect, and religion. Attempts to unify the different groups met with success only rarely. In the 4th century B.C.E., the Maurya Empire united much of the country. Asoka, one of its greatest rulers, became a Buddhist, and the practice of Buddhism spread widely during his time.

During the 4th and 5th centuries C.E., the Gupta Empire brought peace and prosperity, a time when science, literature, and the arts enjoyed a golden age. Another unifying effort began with the Delhi Sultanate, about 1200, which established Islam in India. The followers of Islam, the religion of Mohammed (570-632 C.E.), are called Muslims. Islam spread under the influence of the Mogul Empire, proclaimed in 1526.

Britain, starting in 1639 through the British East India Company, gradually increased its economic influence until it made India a colony in 1858. The Indian independence movement began almost immediately, ending in 1947 when the world recognized two countries — India (primarily Hindu) and Pakistan (primarily Muslim). In 1972, East Pakistan became the separate nation of Bangladesh.

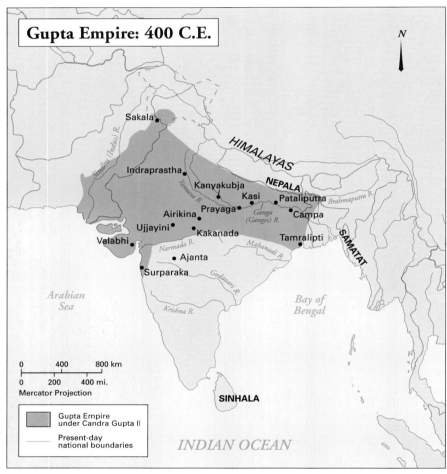

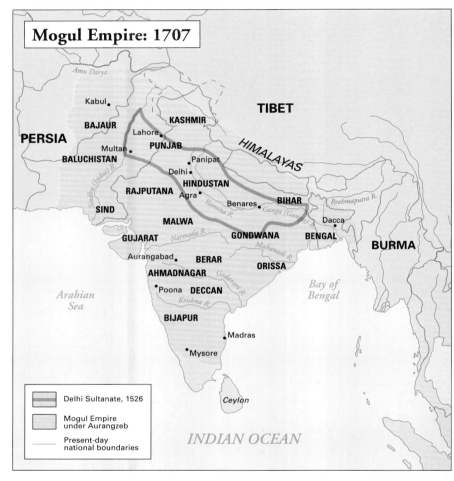

◄ Ajanta, in the northern part of the Deccan Plateau, was an important Buddhist pilgrimage site. This wall painting from the sandstone caves was probably created between 300 and 500 C.E.

► The Taj Mahal is at Agra, in northern India. It is the mausoleum, or burial place, of Mumtaz Mahal, who was married to the Mogul Emperor Shah Jahan. When his wife died in 1629, the emperor ordered the mausoleum built in her memory. The outside is of white marble, inlaid with semi-precious stones, floral designs, and arabesques. The building took eighteen years to complete.

QUICK FACTS   The Moguls ruled over 150 000 000 people.   Arabic numerals are actually Indian in origin.
Indian mathematicians developed the concept of zero.   Indian scientists first stated that the world was round.

47

British traders first arrived in India in the early 17th century. Over the next 200 years, the British East India Company gained control of more and more of the country. From 1858, the British government ruled India directly until that nation was partitioned into two separate independent countries — India and Pakistan — in 1947.

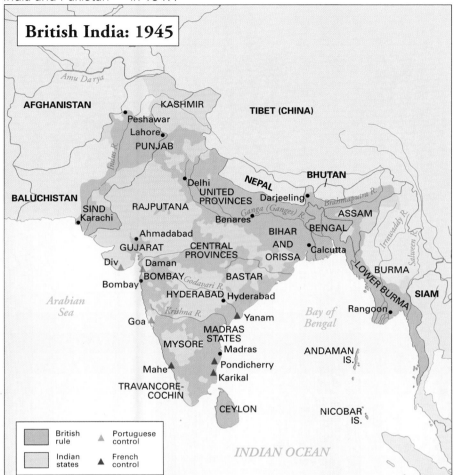

British India: 1945

British rule	▲ Portuguese control
Indian states	▲ French control

Timeline

2500 B.C.E.–1500 B.C.E.	Indus River valley civilization flourishes
1500 B.C.E.	Aryan invasions begin
567 B.C.E.	Siddhartha Gautama, founder of Buddhism, is born
322 B.C.E.–185 B.C.E.	Maurya Empire
273 B.C.E.–232 B.C.E.	Asoka rules the Maurya Empire
320 C.E.–467 C.E.	Gupta Empire — India's "Golden Age"
1206	Muslim rule is established under the Delhi Sultanate
1469	Guru Nanak, founder of the Sikh religion, is born
1498	First European trader/explorer, the Portuguese Vasco da Gama, arrives
1526–1707	Mogul Empire
1639	The British are granted their first trading post — Madras
1757	British East India Company defeats the Muslim ruler of Bengal in the Battle of Plassey
1857–1859	Indian soldiers rebel against the British in the Sepoy Mutiny
1858	India becomes a colony of the British Empire
1885	Beginning of the independence movement — National Congress party is founded
1930–1932	The independence movement encourages civil disobedience against British rule
1947	India and Pakistan gain independence

Queen Victoria reigned from 1837–1901, during the height of the British Empire. The Victoria Memorial in Calcutta is a reminder of the time when India was considered the "brightest jewel in the crown" of Britain.

Jawaharlal Nehru (1889–1964) was one of the leaders of India's struggle for independence, and became the first prime minister when it was gained in 1947. Later, his daughter, Indira Gandhi, served as India's prime minister from 1966–1977, and again from 1980–1984. In turn, Indira's son, Rajiv Gandhi, was prime minister from 1984–1989.

◄ Mohandas Karamchand "Mahatma" Gandhi (1869–1948) is regarded as the "father" of independent India. A believer in nonviolence, he spent more than 30 years struggling to win India's independence from Britain. Gandhi was greatly troubled by the violence that resulted from the partition of British India into India and Pakistan in 1947. He was assassinated in 1948.

The Crossroads of Asia

Southeast Asia is diverse in its geography, peoples, languages, and beliefs. More than fourteen different languages are spoken in the region. As well, more than nine major religions are practiced there. There are over twenty different ethnic groups who live in Southeast Asia.

The area is also divided by its geography. There are numerous mountain ranges, and thousands of islands. The mainland has many hills and valleys.

This region is the crossroads of Asia. Traders, explorers, and invaders have all passed this way. Spices, foods, and wood made the area a target for countries looking to build empires and gain riches. From 1500 till 1945, the world's most powerful nations fought each other for control of the region.

Since World War II ended in 1945, Southeast Asia has suffered through many local wars, and seen much civil strife.

Rice, grown in paddies like these shown here, is the staple food of Southeast Asia.

Buddhist temples are a common sight in many parts of Southeast Asia.

Note:
(1) Every country decides the exact size of its national flag. There is no "standard" measurement used, so each could be different. The flags shown here are not drawn to scale.
(2) Currency rates are mid-1994 figures.

1 cm on this map is equal to 227 km on the ground

| 0 | 500 | 1000 km |

| 0 | 300 | 600 mi. |

1 in. on this map is equal to 363 mi. on the ground
Mercator Projection

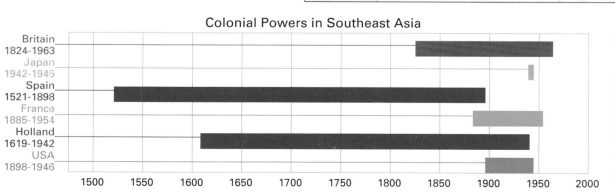

Colonial Powers in Southeast Asia

Britain 1824-1963
Japan 1942-1945
Spain 1521-1898
France 1885-1954
Holland 1619-1942
USA 1898-1946

1500 1550 1600 1650 1700 1750 1800 1850 1900 1950 2000

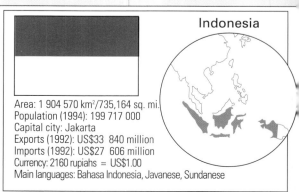

Indonesia

Area: 1 904 570 km²/735,164 sq. mi.
Population (1994): 199 717 000
Capital city: Jakarta
Exports (1992): US$33 840 million
Imports (1992): US$27 606 million
Currency: 2160 rupiahs = US$1.00
Main languages: Bahasa Indonesia, Javanese, Sundanese

QUICK FACTS
The average annual precipitation in some rainforests
can be as much as 10 000 mm (390 in.).

Thailand is the world's largest rice exporter.
Southeast Asia covers an area of approximately 4.5 million km² (1.7 million sq. mi.).
Singapore is slightly less than 3.5 times the size of Washington, D.C.

49

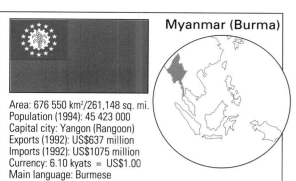

Myanmar (Burma)

Area: 676 550 km²/261,148 sq. mi.
Population (1994) 45 423 000
Capital city: Yangon (Rangoon)
Exports (1992): US$637 million
Imports (1992): US$1075 million
Currency: 6.10 kyats = US$1.00
Main language: Burmese

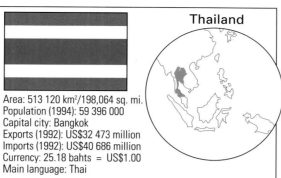

Thailand

Area: 513 120 km²/198,064 sq. mi.
Population (1994): 59 396 000
Capital city: Bangkok
Exports (1992): US$32 473 million
Imports (1992): US$40 686 million
Currency: 25.18 bahts = US$1.00
Main language: Thai

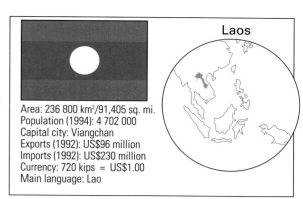

Laos

Area: 236 800 km²/91,405 sq. mi.
Population (1994) 4 702 000
Capital city: Viangchan
Exports (1992): US$96 million
Imports (1992): US$230 million
Currency: 720 kips = US$1.00
Main language: Lao

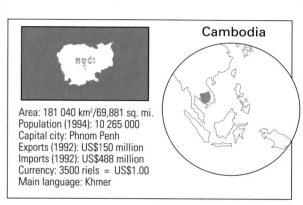

Cambodia

Area: 181 040 km²/69,881 sq. mi.
Population (1994): 10 265 000
Capital city: Phnom Penh
Exports (1992): US$150 million
Imports (1992): US$488 million
Currency: 3500 riels = US$1.00
Main language: Khmer

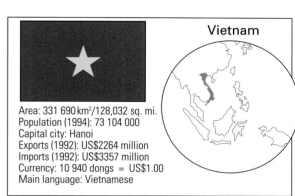

Vietnam

Area: 331 690 km²/128,032 sq. mi.
Population (1994): 73 104 000
Capital city: Hanoi
Exports (1992): US$2264 million
Imports (1992): US$3357 million
Currency: 10 940 dongs = US$1.00
Main language: Vietnamese

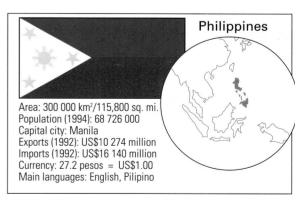

Philippines

Area: 300 000 km²/115,800 sq. mi.
Population (1994): 68 726 000
Capital city: Manila
Exports (1992): US$10 274 million
Imports (1992): US$16 140 million
Currency: 27.2 pesos = US$1.00
Main languages: English, Pilipino

Southeast Asia

★ Capital city
■ Over 5 000 000
■ 1 000 000–5 000 000
● 100 000–1 000 000

TAIWAN

Philippine Sea

Quezon City
Manila
PHILIPPINES

Visayan Is.
● Cebu

● Cagayan de Oro
Mindanao
Davao

PACIFIC OCEAN

Manado

Molucca Is.

Ambon

Banda Sea

New Guinea
PAPUA NEW GUINEA

INDONESIA

Lesser Sunda Is. Timor

Arafura Sea

130° E   140° E   150° E
AUSTRALIA

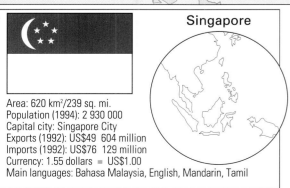

Singapore

Area: 620 km²/239 sq. mi.
Population (1994): 2 930 000
Capital city: Singapore City
Exports (1992): US$49 604 million
Imports (1992): US$76 129 million
Currency: 1.55 dollars = US$1.00
Main languages: Bahasa Malaysia, English, Mandarin, Tamil

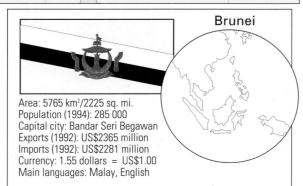

Brunei

Area: 5765 km²/2225 sq. mi.
Population (1994): 285 000
Capital city: Bandar Seri Begawan
Exports (1992): US$2365 million
Imports (1992): US$2281 million
Currency: 1.55 dollars = US$1.00
Main languages: Malay, English

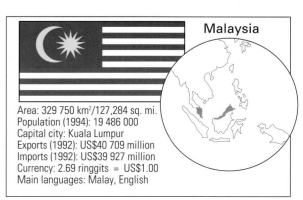

Malaysia

Area: 329 750 km²/127,284 sq. mi.
Population (1994): 19 486 000
Capital city: Kuala Lumpur
Exports (1992): US$40 709 million
Imports (1992): US$39 927 million
Currency: 2.69 ringgits = US$1.00
Main languages: Malay, English

The Ancient Capital of the Khmers

Angkor was the capital city of the Khmer people of Cambodia from the 9th–15th centuries C.E. The city was built around a temple on a hill that symbolized the mountain standing at the center of the world, according to Hindu belief. Over the centuries, Angkor grew as other temples were built. Large reservoirs that were used for irrigation were also built.

The most famous of the Angkor temple complexes is Angkor Wat, built during the 12th century. It is a huge rectangle, almost 1 km^2 (0.39 sq. mi.) in area, and is encircled by a moat that is 20 m (66 ft.) wide. Inside are several walled courtyards that surround a central pyramid with five graceful, lotus-shaped towers. The intricately carved stone walls and towers bear images from both Buddhism and Hinduism.

The city of Angkor was abandoned in 1434. Soon, the jungle took over, and Angkor was "lost" for nearly 450 years. It was rediscovered in 1861 by a French explorer. For the following century, Angkor became a popular destination for both tourists and archaeologists. Then, in 1970, civil war virtually closed Cambodia to the outside world. Sadly, the ruins were damaged during the war.

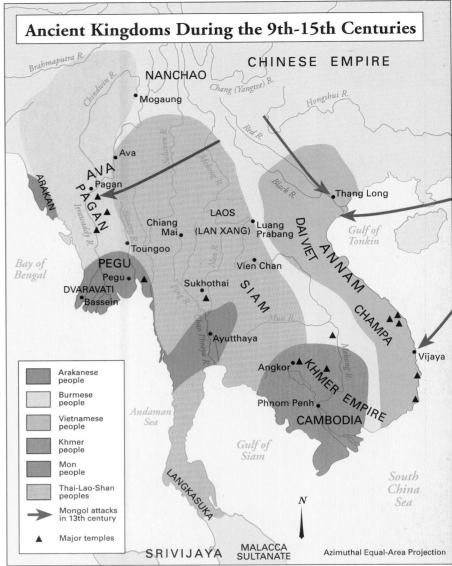

Ancient Kingdoms During the 9th-15th Centuries

■	Arakanese people
□	Burmese people
■	Vietnamese people
■	Khmer people
■	Mon people
■	Thai-Lao-Shan peoples
→	Mongol attacks in 13th century
▲	Major temples

Azimuthal Equal-Area Projection

◄ After Angkor was abandoned, the city was forgotten about for nearly 450 years. When it was rediscovered, archaeologists began excavations to uncover it. They were able to learn a great deal about Hindu and Buddhist art and architecture.

Plan of Central Wat

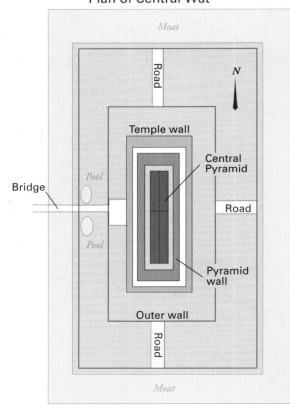

The walls of Angkor Wat are carved with figures and stories from both Hinduism and Buddhism. Both religions had reached Cambodia nearly 1000 years before the temple complex was built.

▼ The design of Angkor Wat is a "map" of the Hindu view of the universe.

QUICK FACTS There are more than 400 Buddhist temples and monasteries in Bangkok. Bangkok is a 12 288-km (7637-mi.) flight from Los Angeles. By the year 2000, the city's population is expected to be over 7.5 million.

51

A Major Metropolis

Bangkok, capital of Thailand, is a political, religious, and economic center whose life revolves around the Chao Phraya River. With a population of approximately six million people, the city is the largest in Thailand.

There are tremendous traffic jams and a serious air pollution problem in Bangkok. But the city is filled with splendid temples, as well as many other fascinating religious and cultural sites. Thousands of tourists visit every year, and tourism is an important part of Thailand's economy.

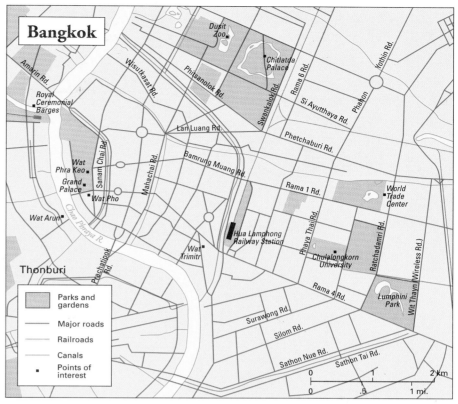

Bangkok

Parks and gardens
Major roads
Railroads
Canals
Points of interest

Thonburi

Bangkok lies on the east bank of the Chao Phraya River. Thonburi, located on the west side of the river, is considered to be part of metropolitan Bangkok.

Thailand has more Buddhist wats, or temples, per person than any other country in the world. Around Bangkok, there is often one in sight. This photograph is of Wat Arun, the Temple of Dawn.

Until the introduction of automobiles, the river was the "main street", not only for Bangkok, but also for most of Thailand. It still plays an important role in Bangkok's transportation system today.

Because of heavy traffic, air pollution is a major problem in Bangkok. The city is home to 90% of all the motor vehicles in Thailand.

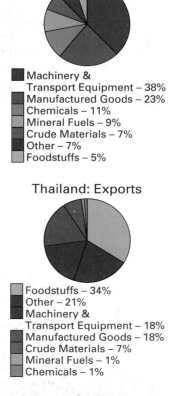

Thailand: Imports

- Machinery & Transport Equipment – 38%
- Manufactured Goods – 23%
- Chemicals – 11%
- Mineral Fuels – 9%
- Crude Materials – 7%
- Other – 7%
- Foodstuffs – 5%

Thailand: Exports

- Foodstuffs – 34%
- Other – 21%
- Machinery & Transport Equipment – 18%
- Manufactured Goods – 18%
- Crude Materials – 7%
- Mineral Fuels – 1%
- Chemicals – 1%

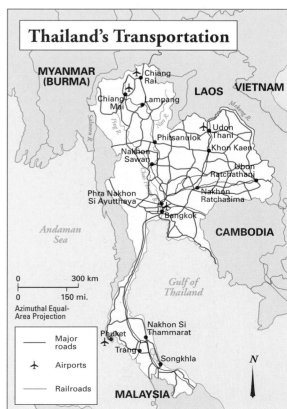

Thailand's Transportation

MYANMAR (BURMA)
LAOS
VIETNAM
Chiang Rai
Chiang Mai
Lampang
Phitsanulok
Udon Thani
Khon Kaen
Nakhon Sawan
Ubon Ratchathani
Phra Nakhon Si Ayutthaya
Nakhon Ratchasima
Bangkok
CAMBODIA
Andaman Sea
Gulf of Thailand
Phuket
Nakhon Si Thammarat
Trang
Songkhla
MALAYSIA

0   300 km
0   150 mi.
Azimuthal Equal-Area Projection

Major roads
Airports
Railroads

N

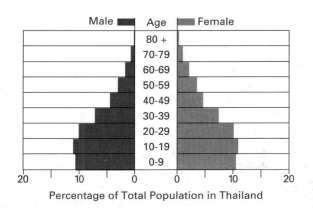

Male   Age   Female
80 +
70-79
60-69
50-59
40-49
30-39
20-29
10-19
0-9

20   10   0   0   10   20

Percentage of Total Population in Thailand

A Land of Volcanoes

Indonesia is made up of more than 13 000 islands that stretch in an arc along the Equator. Java, one of the larger islands, has only 7% of Indonesia's total land area, yet it is home to more than 60% of its almost 200 million people. Jakarta, Indonesia's capital, is one of the most densely populated cities in the world. In contrast, many of the smaller Indonesian islands are completely uninhabited.

Indonesia is a land of volcanoes. There are more than 100 on Java alone, including 17 that are still active. Volcanic cones are dotted regularly across the island. The fertile volcanic soils of this island are good for growing food, one reason for its high population density.

Indonesia's economy is based on oil and gas production, manufacturing, tourism, and farming. Improved farming methods and regular enriching of the soils by volcanic eruptions enable Indonesia's farmers to grow enough food for the country's needs.

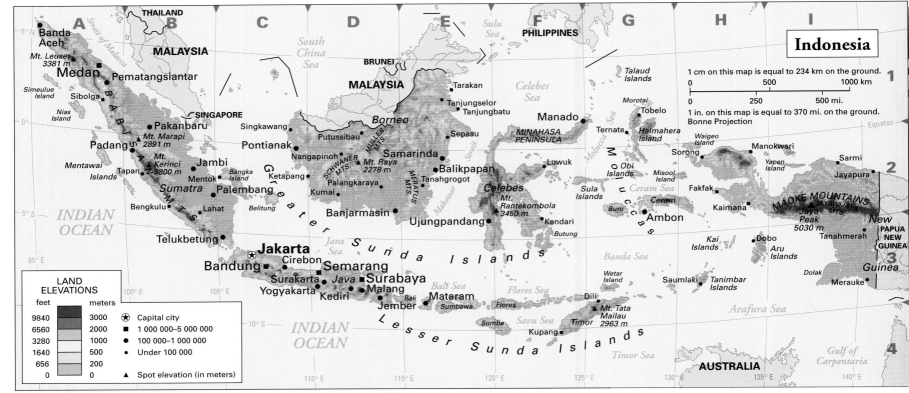

Borobudur is the largest Buddhist monument in the world. It lies right at the heart of Java, not far from Yogyakarta. Archaeologists believe that it took 10 000 workers at least 25 years to build the shrine.

Indonesia is located where two of the earth's tectonic plates meet. The result is the many volcanoes that are found throughout the country.

Major Indonesian Crops

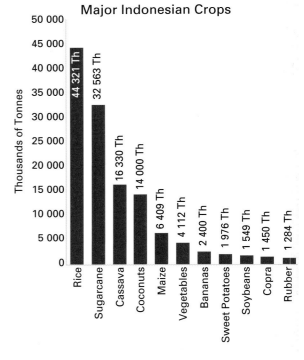

Crop	Thousands of Tonnes
Rice	44 321 Th
Sugarcane	32 563 Th
Cassava	16 330 Th
Coconuts	14 000 Th
Maize	6 409 Th
Vegetables	4 112 Th
Bananas	2 400 Th
Sweet Potatoes	1 976 Th
Soybeans	1 549 Th
Copra	1 450 Th
Rubber	1 284 Th

Fishing is an important activity in Indonesia. Fishing villages are located along rivers and on the coast.

The mangrove swamps found on the coast are important to Indonesia's ecology. Silt is trapped in amongst the mangroves and builds up over time, resulting in increasing land area. The swamps are endangered by pollution from industry and other human activity.

QUICK FACTS

Languages: Bahasa Indonesia, Javanese, Sundanese
Area: 1 904 570 km² (735,164 sq. mi.)
Population (1994): 199 717 000

Imports (1992): US$27 606 million
Exports (1992): US$33 840 million

53

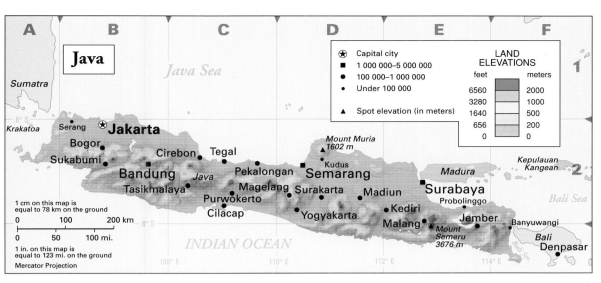

Java's land shortage and mountainous terrain have forced people to maximize land use. Mountainside terraces are one strategy used by farmers to get the most production from steep hillsides.

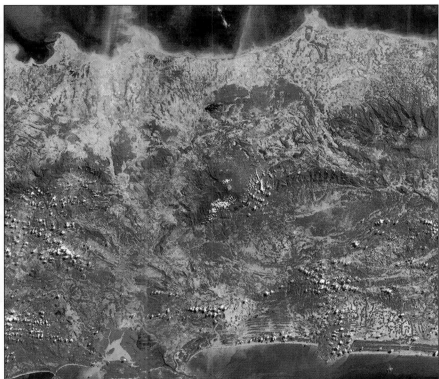

This Landsat photograph shows central Java. The satellite uses infra-red photography, which is sensitive to heat. The red areas show healthy vegetation, while the blue is water or wetland.

Jakarta, Indonesia's capital, may be the most densely populated city in the world. Estimates for 1995 said it was home to 11 151 000 people. It covers an area of approximately 197 km² (76 sq. mi.).

Population Density of Selected Indonesian Islands

	Population Density	
	People/km²	People/sq. mi.
Java	750.7	1944.2
Bali	499.5	1293.9
Celebes	66.2	171.4
Borneo	16.9	43.7
New Guinea	3.9	10.1
All Indonesia	93.4	242.0

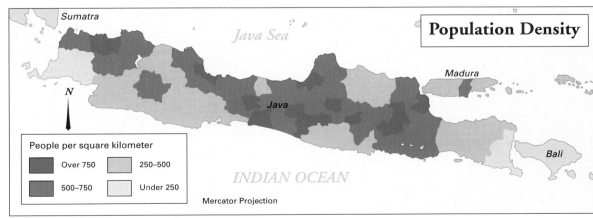

Population Density

People per square kilometer

Over 750
500–750
250–500
Under 250

Mercator Projection

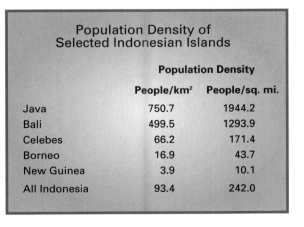

Land Use

Rice crops
Tree crops
Other crops
Fish ponds
Shifting agriculture
Forest
Urban regions

Mercator Projection

Land Use in Indonesia

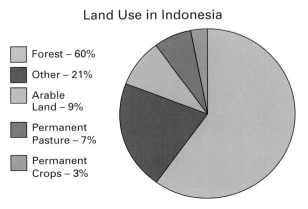

Forest – 60%
Other – 21%
Arable Land – 9%
Permanent Pasture – 7%
Permanent Crops – 3%

QUICK FACTS
Languages: Pilipino and English
Area: 300 000 km² (115,800 sq.mi.)
Population (1994): 68 726 000
Imports (1992): US$16 140 million
Exports (1992): US$10 274 million

A Country of Islands

The Republic of the Philippines is made up of 7000 islands. Fewer than half the islands have names and only about 900 of them are inhabited.

The ancestors of today's Filipinos came from Indonesia and Malaysia. They created small, isolated communities throughout the islands. As a result, the Philippines has a wide variety of customs, languages, and ways of life.

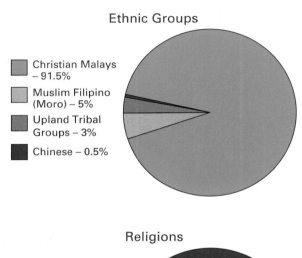

Rice grows well in the warm, moist climate of the Philippines. In recent years, new high-yielding varieties of rice have aided efficient terracing in feeding a growing population.

Ethnic Groups

- Christian Malays – 91.5%
- Muslim Filipino (Moro) – 5%
- Upland Tribal Groups – 3%
- Chinese – 0.5%

Religions

- Christianity – 88%
- Aglipayanism – 6%
- Islam – 4%
- Other – 2%

Manila, capital city of the Philippines, is the nation's largest city and busiest port. It is a major center of trade, industry, and commerce. Like other cities in developing nations, it is growing rapidly as many of the country's rural poor come to seek work and a better standard of living.

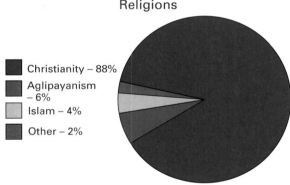

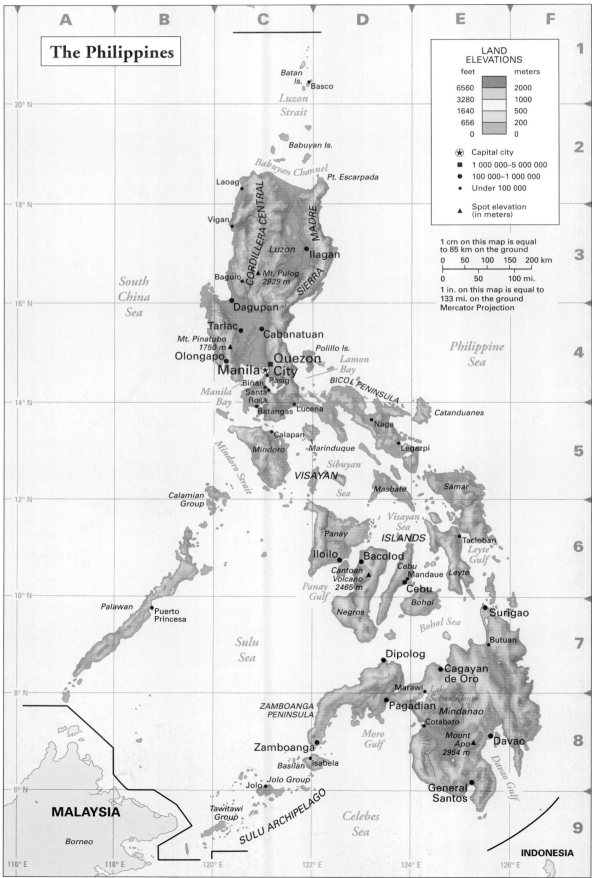

The Philippines

LAND ELEVATIONS

feet	meters
6560	2000
3280	1000
1640	500
656	200
0	0

⊛ Capital city
■ 1 000 000–5 000 000
● 100 000–1 000 000
• Under 100 000

▲ Spot elevation (in meters)

1 cm on this map is equal to 85 km on the ground

0 50 100 150 200 km
0   50   100 mi.

1 in. on this map is equal to 133 mi. on the ground
Mercator Projection

Batan Is.
Basco
Luzon Strait
Babuyan Is.
Babuyan Channel
Laoag
Pt. Escarpada
Vigan
CORDILLERA CENTRAL
MADRE
Luzon
Ilagan
Baguio
Mt. Pulog 2929 m
SIERRA
South China Sea
Dagupan
Tarlac
Cabanatuan
Mt. Pinatubo 1750 m
Polillo Is.
Olongapo
Quezon City
Lamon Bay
Manila
Biñan Pasig
BICOL PENINSULA
Manila Bay
Santa Rosa
Batangas Lucena
Calapan
Nage
Catanduanes
Mindoro
Marinduque
Legazpi
Mindoro Strait
Sibuyan Sea
VISAYAN
Masbate
Samar
Calamian Group
Visayan Sea
Panay
ISLANDS
Tacloban
Iloilo
Bacolod
Leyte Gulf
Cantoan Volcano 2465 m
Cebu
Mandaue Leyte
Panay Gulf
Cebu
Bohol
Palawan
Negros
Surigao
Puerto Princesa
Bohol Sea
Butuan
Sulu Sea
Dipolog
Cagayan de Oro
Marawi
Lake Sultan Alonto
ZAMBOANGA PENINSULA
Pagadian
Mindanao
Cotabato
Zamboanga
Moro Gulf
Mount Apo 2954 m
Davao
Basilan Isabela
Jolo Group
Jolo
General Santos
Davao Gulf
MALAYSIA
Tawitawi Group
SULU ARCHIPELAGO
Celebes Sea
Borneo
INDONESIA
Philippine Sea

South China Sea
Sulu Sea

QUICK FACTS
Languages: English, Bahasa Malaysia, Mandarin, Tamil
Area: 620 km² (239 sq. mi.)

Population (1994): 2 930 000
Imports (1992): US$76 129 million
Exports (1992): US$49 604 million

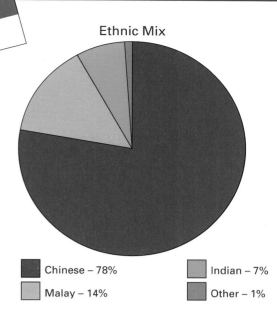

A City State

Singapore is an independent nation, with its own government, army, and national airline. It consists of Singapore Island and more than 50 smaller islands, many of them uninhabited. Almost all of the people live in the capital, Singapore City.

Thanks to its location, Singapore is a global crossroads in the fast-growing Pacific Rim trading network. It is a crowded, bustling center of trade, finance, and manufacturing, and is one of the most prosperous countries in Asia.

Ethnic Mix

- Chinese – 78%
- Malay – 14%
- Indian – 7%
- Other – 1%

▼ The streets of Singapore reflect the cosmopolitan population of the country.

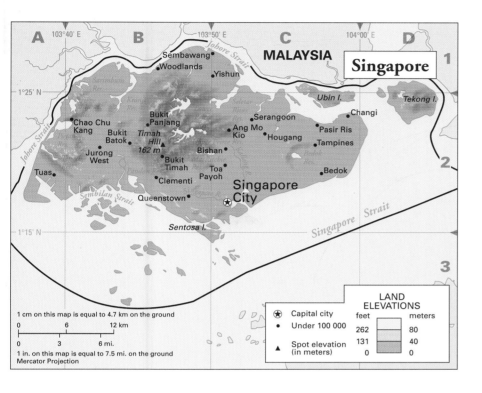

1 cm on this map is equal to 4.7 km on the ground
0   6   12 km
0   3   6 mi.
1 in. on this map is equal to 7.5 mi. on the ground
Mercator Projection

LAND ELEVATIONS
	feet	meters
	262	80
	131	40
	0	0

✪ Capital city
● Under 100 000
▲ Spot elevation (in meters)

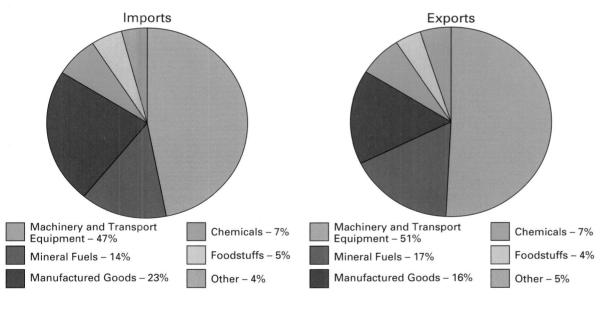

Imports

- Machinery and Transport Equipment – 47%
- Mineral Fuels – 14%
- Manufactured Goods – 23%
- Chemicals – 7%
- Foodstuffs – 5%
- Other – 4%

Exports

- Machinery and Transport Equipment – 51%
- Mineral Fuels – 17%
- Manufactured Goods – 16%
- Chemicals – 7%
- Foodstuffs – 4%
- Other – 5%

The orchid is the national flower of Singapore. Orchids from Singapore are exported to western Europe, Japan, Australia, and the United States.

Singapore is one of the busiest ports in the Pacific Rim. In 1991, it handled more than 200 million tonnes (197 million tons) of cargo.

With a 1994 population of 2 930 000, Singapore had a population density of 4725.8 people/km² (12,259.4/sq. mi.).

Singapore's ethnic groups create a variety of cultures within the country. This photo shows a Malay wedding.

An Economic Giant

Hong Kong is an important center of trade, finance, manufacturing, and tourism. Even though it occupies only a small area of land, Hong Kong is an economic giant whose influence is felt worldwide.

Until the mid 1800s, Hong Kong was part of China. In 1842, it was absorbed into the British Empire when Great Britain occupied Hong Kong Island. Then, in 1860, the Kowloon Peninsula came under British control. Finally, in 1898, the New Territories became part of what we now know as Hong Kong. China and Britain signed a 99-year lease for this area. In 1984, the two signed an agreement which means that in 1997 Hong Kong once more becomes part of China.

Today, Hong Kong is one of the most densely populated areas in the world. Partly because of the large supply of low-paid labor, there are many light manufacturing industries that produce a wide range of goods. The biggest industry is textile making.

Clothes, plastics, and electronic goods are also manufactured in Hong Kong and exported all over the world.

Because the colony is so small and so crowded, there is little land available for farming, and real estate prices are very high. Nearly all food and water has to be imported.

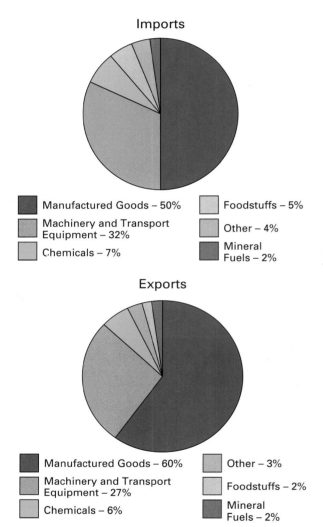

Imports

- Manufactured Goods – 50%
- Machinery and Transport Equipment – 32%
- Chemicals – 7%
- Foodstuffs – 5%
- Other – 4%
- Mineral Fuels – 2%

Exports

- Manufactured Goods – 60%
- Machinery and Transport Equipment – 27%
- Chemicals – 6%
- Other – 3%
- Foodstuffs – 2%
- Mineral Fuels – 2%

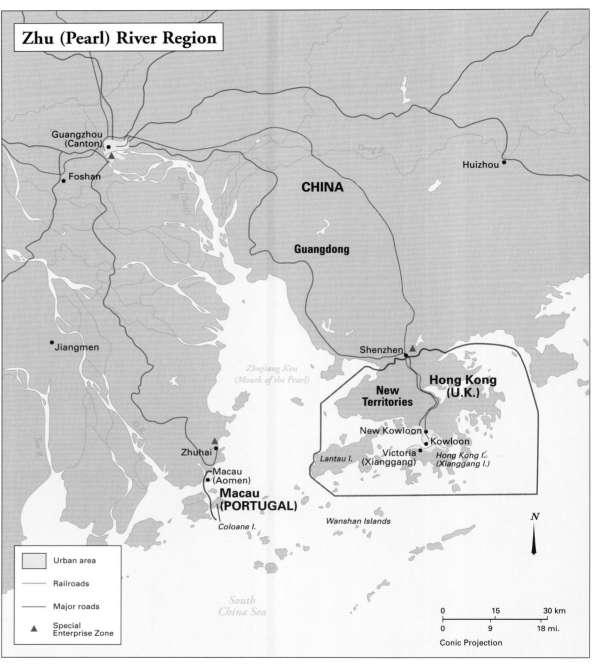

Zhu (Pearl) River Region

Guangzhou (Canton)
Foshan
Dong R.
Huizhou
CHINA
Guangdong
Jiangmen
Shenzhen
Zhujiang Kou (Mouth of the Pearl)
Hong Kong (U.K.)
New Territories
New Kowloon
Kowloon
Lantau I.
Victoria (Xianggang)
Hong Kong I. (Xianggang I.)
Zhuhai
Macau (Aomen)
Macau (PORTUGAL)
Wanshan Islands
Coloane I.
South China Sea

Legend:
- Urban area
- Railroads
- Major roads
- ▲ Special Enterprise Zone

0 15 30 km
0 9 18 mi.
Conic Projection

N

Victoria Harbour separates Hong Kong Island and the Kowloon Peninsula. It is one of the busiest harbors in the world. In 1991, more than 100 million tonnes (98 million tons) of cargo passed through Hong Kong.

Textiles and clothing are exported all over the world and are an important part of Hong Kong's economy. The colony is famous for its skilled tailors, who can produce a made-to-measure suit in a day.

Hong Kong is the busiest container port in the world. Most of the products manufactured in the colony are shipped by sea to Europe or North America.

QUICK FACTS
Languages: Cantonese and English
Area: 1040 km² (402 sq. mi.)

Population (1994): 5 847 000
Imports (1992): US$123 430 million
Exports (1992): US$119 512 million

57

Hong Kong is one of the most crowded places in the world. The population density is 5622.1 people/km² (14,544.8/sq. mi.).

With trade, finance, and tourism having a great impact on life in Hong Kong, scenes like this are common.

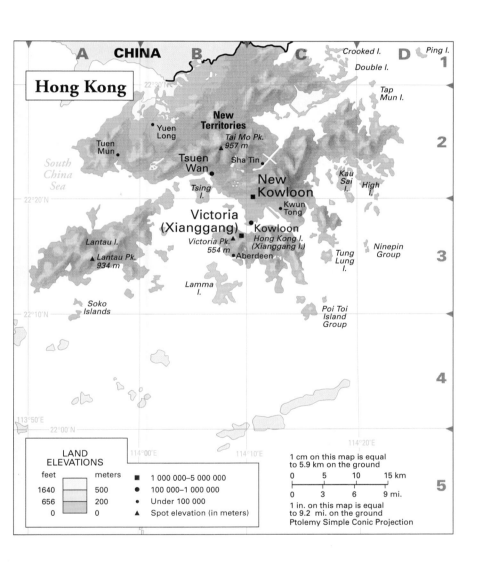

Trade per Person

	US$
USA	3.83
Germany	10.31
Japan	4.58
France	8.23
UK	7.04
Italy	6.49
Netherlands	17.49
Canada	8.97
Belgium/Luxembourg	23.71
Hong Kong	31.67

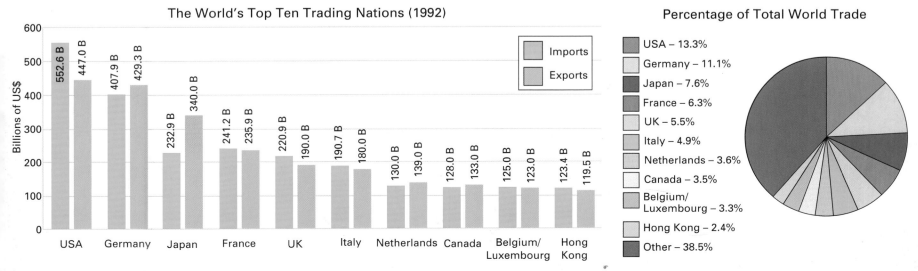

The World's Top Ten Trading Nations (1992)

Billions of US$

Imports / Exports

Nation	Imports	Exports
USA	552.6 B	447.0 B
Germany	407.9 B	429.3 B
Japan	232.9 B	340.0 B
France	241.2 B	235.9 B
UK	220.9 B	190.0 B
Italy	190.7 B	180.0 B
Netherlands	130.0 B	139.0 B
Canada	128.0 B	133.0 B
Belgium/Luxembourg	125.0 B	123.0 B
Hong Kong	123.4 B	119.5 B

Percentage of Total World Trade

- USA – 13.3%
- Germany – 11.1%
- Japan – 7.6%
- France – 6.3%
- UK – 5.5%
- Italy – 4.9%
- Netherlands – 3.6%
- Canada – 3.5%
- Belgium/Luxembourg – 3.3%
- Hong Kong – 2.4%
- Other – 38.5%

The Most Populous Country

With more than one billion people, China has the largest population of any country. One person in every five alive today resides in China. Most live in the densely settled North China Plain or the Chang (Yangtze) River Delta and Plain.

China is the world's third largest country by area. Spread across this vast land are many different natural environments. Tibet stretches from the northern side of the Himalayas across the Tibetan Plateau, while the dry, windswept Taklimakan and Gobi Deserts cover much of northern China. The northeastern part of the country is forest-covered, cold in winter, and rich in mineral deposits.

The hills and valleys of southeast China have a climate that is warm and moist for most of the year. Rice is cultivated in the valleys, while the hillsides are covered by subtropical forests.

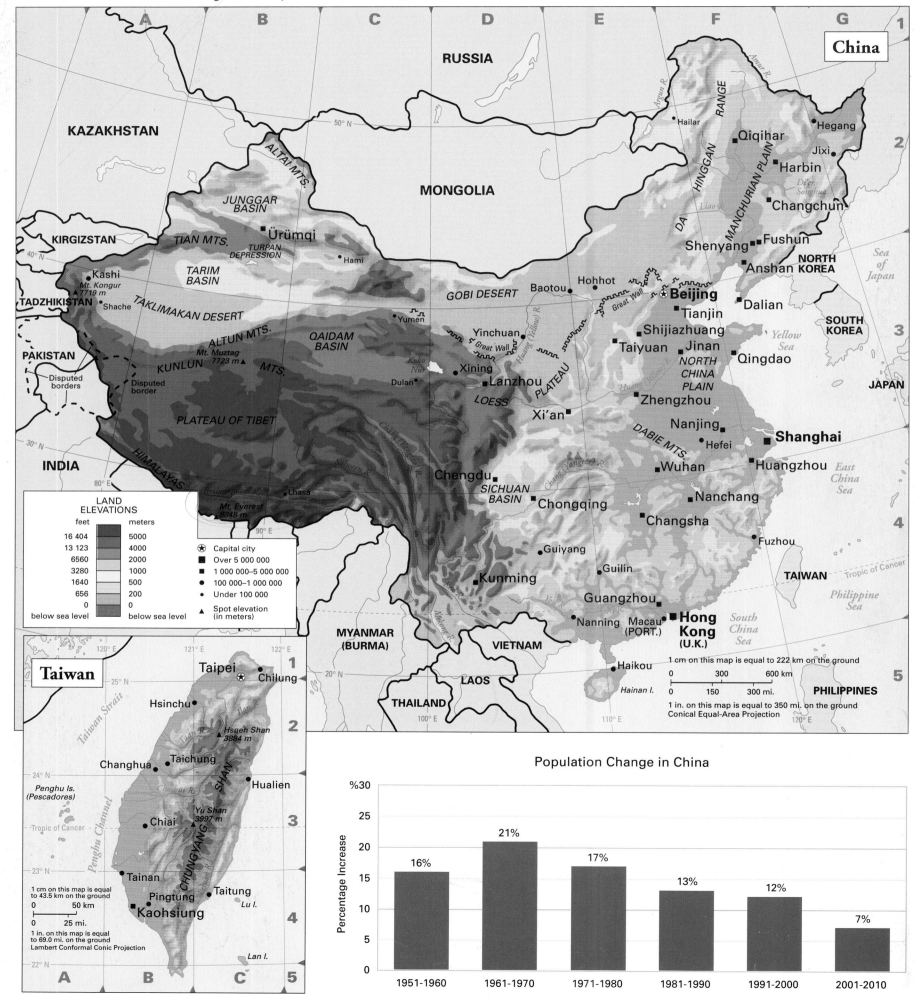

China

LAND ELEVATIONS

feet	meters
16 404	5000
13 123	4000
6560	2000
3280	1000
1640	500
656	200
0	0
below sea level	below sea level

☆ Capital city
■ Over 5 000 000
■ 1 000 000–5 000 000
● 100 000–1 000 000
• Under 100 000
▲ Spot elevation (in meters)

1 cm on this map is equal to 222 km on the ground
0   300   600 km
0   150   300 mi.
1 in. on this map is equal to 350 mi. on the ground
Conical Equal-Area Projection

Taiwan

1 cm on this map is equal to 43.5 km on the ground
0   50 km
0   25 mi.
1 in. on this map is equal to 69.0 mi. on the ground
Lambert Conformal Conic Projection

Population Change in China

Percentage Increase / %30

Period	Percentage Increase
1951-1960	16%
1961-1970	21%
1971-1980	17%
1981-1990	13%
1991-2000	12%
2001-2010	7%

QUICK FACTS
Languages: Mandarin, Wu, Cantonese, Xiang, Min, Hakka
Area: 9 596 960 km² (3,704,427 sq. mi.)

Population (1994): 1 192 000 000
Imports (1992): US$81 739 million
Exports (1992): US$86 220 million

59

Population Density

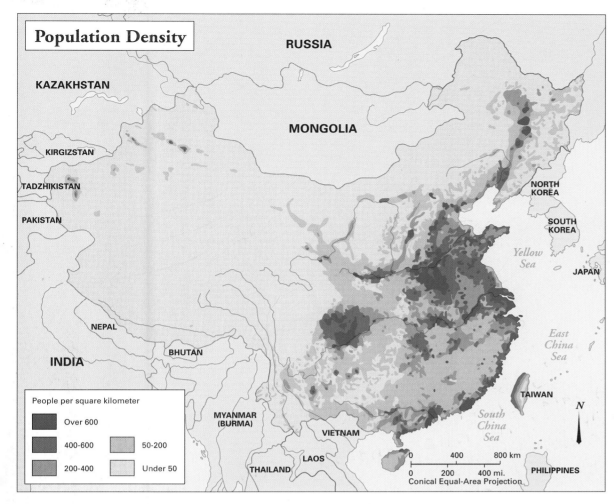

China has more cities of one million people or more than any other country in the world.

People per square kilometer
- Over 600
- 400-600
- 200-400
- 50-200
- Under 50

Urban/Rural Population

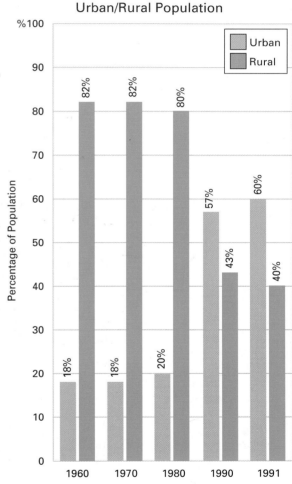

- Urban
- Rural

1960: 18%, 82%
1970: 18%, 82%
1980: 20%, 80%
1990: 57%, 43%
1991: 60%, 40%

The fertile soils of the Chang (Yangtze) River valley and the North China Plain produce the large quantities of wheat, rice, vegetables, and other crops needed to feed hundreds of millions of people.

The cold winters of the Manchurian Plain, the steep rocky slopes of the Himalayas and other Tibetan mountains can support only a small portion of China's population. The dry, windswept Gobi, and other deserts of the northwest, are also sparsely populated regions.

Farming and Food

China has more people to feed than any other nation in the world. It is huge in area, but much of the land is mountainous. Farmers must rely on the fertile soils of the North China Plain, and of the many river valleys, to grow enough food to feed more than one billion people. These soils are some of the richest in the world, and China's farmers use them well. No matter how skilled they are, however, it is still impossible to produce enough food for all. China has to import grain from Canada and other countries.

There are probably more types of foods and ways of cooking them in China than anywhere else on earth. The varying climate, soil, resources, and landscape has resulted in a variety of regional dishes and cooking methods. North of the Chang (Yangtze) River, the staple ingredient used is wheat, or other cereal grains. To the south, where the climate is warmer, rice and vegetables are the basis for most dishes.

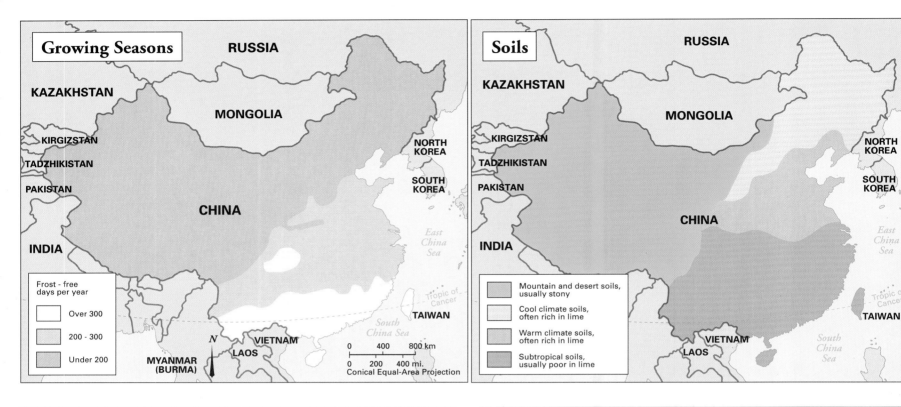

At Haikou, on Hainan Island, market vendors sell all kinds of tropical fruits and vegetables, as well as many animals. Hainan is the most southerly point in China, and the climate is warm and moist.

China produces 580 000 tonnes (571,000 tons) of tea every year. Some of the best tea is grown on the hillsides of Zhejiang Province.

Traditional methods of farming are mixed with more modern ones. On the high Tibetan Plateau, farmers use animals or tractors to pull the plow through their fields.

Wheat must be threshed in order to separate the grain from the stalks. The Chang (Yangtze) River Delta in Jiangsu Province, where this photograph was taken, is the southern limit of China's wheat-growing area.

QUICK FACTS
China has 7% of the world's arable land.
In 1992, China grew 36% of the world's rice.

Urbanization results in the loss of more than 405 000 ha
(1 million acres) of arable land each year.

61

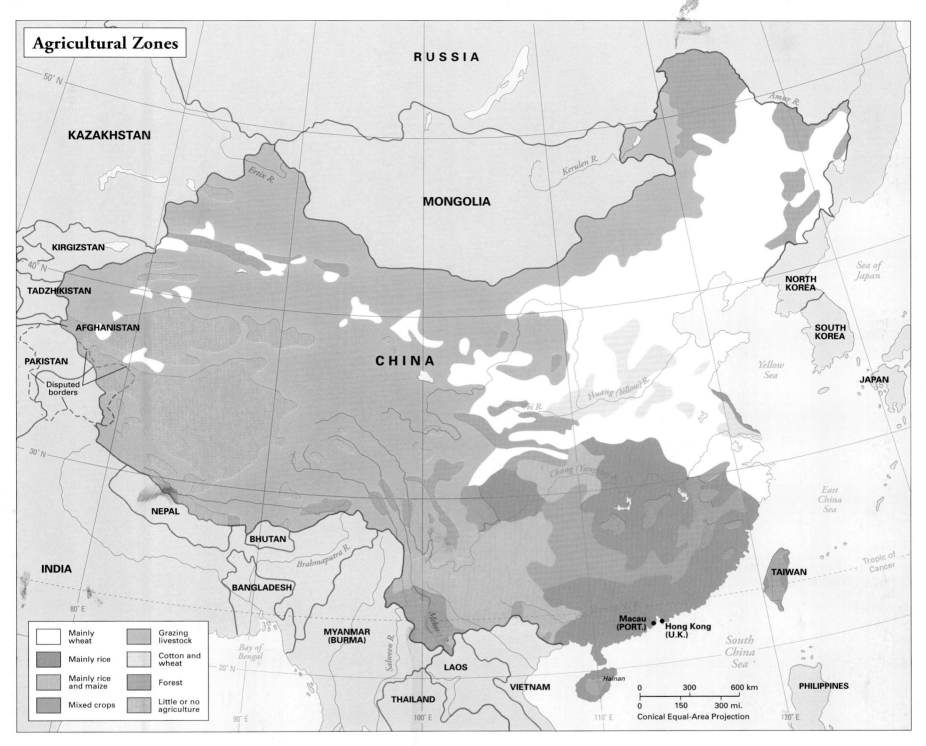

Agricultural Zones

☐ Mainly wheat	☐ Grazing livestock
☐ Mainly rice	☐ Cotton and wheat
☐ Mainly rice and maize	☐ Forest
☐ Mixed crops	☐ Little or no agriculture

Conical Equal-Area Projection

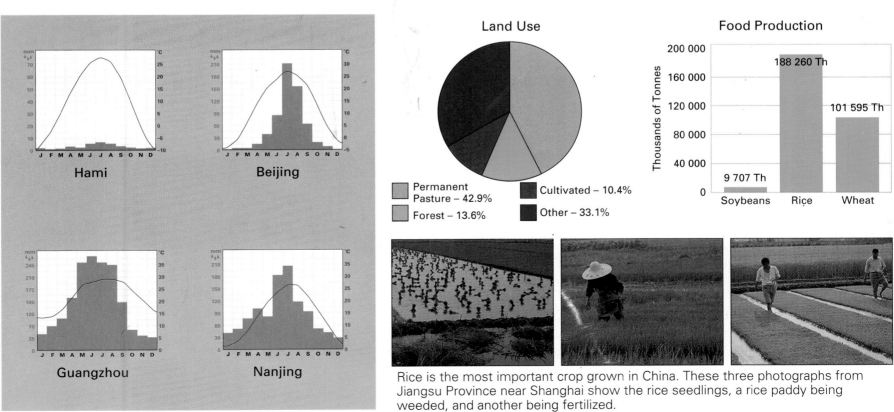

Hami

Beijing

Guangzhou

Nanjing

Land Use

- Permanent Pasture – 42.9%
- Forest – 13.6%
- Cultivated – 10.4%
- Other – 33.1%

Food Production

Thousands of Tonnes

- Soybeans: 9 707 Th
- Rice: 188 260 Th
- Wheat: 101 595 Th

Rice is the most important crop grown in China. These three photographs from Jiangsu Province near Shanghai show the rice seedlings, a rice paddy being weeded, and another being fertilized.

Chinese Tradition

China's history can be traced back almost 4000 years. For much of that time the country was ruled by a succession of dynasties. A dynasty is a series of rulers who come from the same family. Kublai Khan, for example, was the founder of the Yuan Dynasty.

Each dynasty has had its own effect on the culture of present-day China. Some traditions in modern Chinese art go back as far as the Shang Dynasty. Confucius lived more than 2500 years ago, yet his teachings still have a strong influence on Chinese life today. Even foreign rulers, such as the emperors of the Yuan and Qin Dynasties, have respected the deep traditions and values of the country.

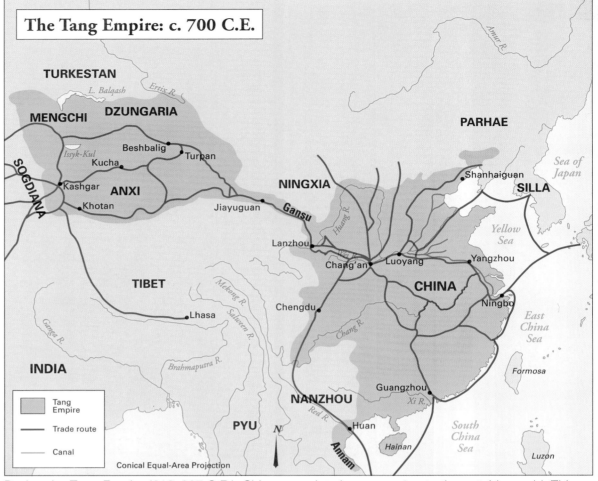

The Tang Empire: c. 700 C.E.

During the Tang Empire (618–907 C.E.), Chinese society became open to the outside world. This was a golden age in China.

The Great Wall was begun in the 3rd century B.C.E. It was built to keep hostile neighbors out of China. It was reconstructed in the 15th century C.E. Most of the wall now lies in ruins.

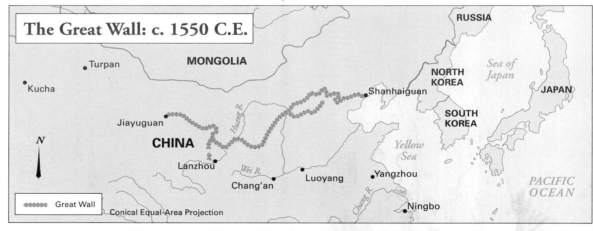

The Great Wall: c. 1550 C.E.

Almost 3500 years ago, the Shang Dynasty (1554–1122 B.C.E.) ruled the Huang (Yellow) River valley. Their craftspeople were highly skilled, and made beautiful ceremonial pieces such as this bronze jar. It would have been used during sacred rituals.

Shi Huangti, emperor during the Qin Dynasty (221–206 B.C.E.), was hated by the people because of his harsh rule. He imposed cruel laws and heavy taxes. Many soldiers and laborers died during the building of the Great Wall. When he grew older, he was afraid he might be assassinated. For this reason, he slept in a different bed, in a different place, every night.

QUICK FACTS
Paper money was used in China as early as 1024 C.E.
Wheelbarrows were invented in China in the 11th century C.E.

Paper was invented in China in the 3rd century B.C.E.
Printing was used in China as early as 1086 C.E.
Gunpowder was invented in China in the 11th century C.E.

63

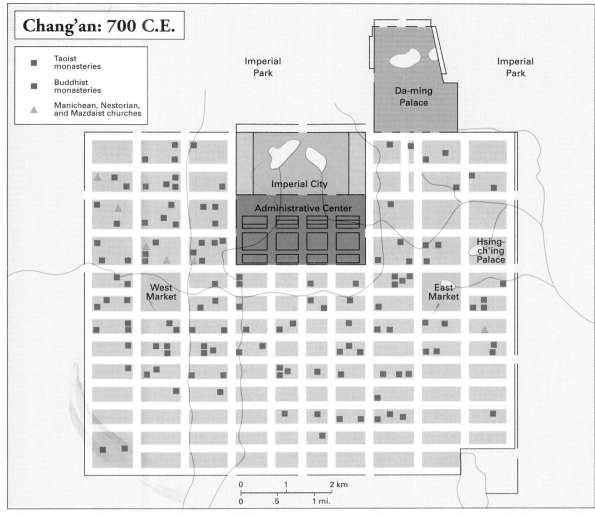

Chang'an: 700 C.E.

- ■ Taoist monasteries
- ■ Buddhist monasteries
- ▲ Manichean, Nestorian, and Mazdaist churches

Imperial Park

Imperial Park

Da-ming Palace

Imperial City

Administrative Center

Hsing-ch'ing Palace

West Market

East Market

0 1 2 km
0 .5 1 mi.

Chang'an, the Tang capital, like many Chinese cities, was carefully planned. Its streets line up with the cardinal directions — north, south, east, and west.

Kublai Khan, a Mongol, ruled from 1260–1294 C.E. Although he was a foreign conqueror, he tried to win the confidence of the Chinese people. He became a Buddhist, and changed his name to Yuan. This was the beginning of the Yuan Dynasty, which lasted until 1368 C.E. Marco Polo visited Kublai Khan's court in 1275.

Confucius (551–479 B.C.E.) is considered by many people to be China's greatest philosopher. He believed that all humans should be judged on their actions rather than on the nobility of their birth. His teachings became a guide both for the rulers of China and for the ordinary people.

The Imperial Palace, built during the Ming Dynasty, is also known as the Forbidden City. Emperor Yong Le wanted the palace to show the harmony that exists between heaven and earth. The Forbidden City is laid out in a rectangular pattern, with the most important buildings at the north end. For 500 years, China was ruled from here. Today, the Forbidden City is a museum.

The Ming Dynasty (1368–1644 C.E.) was a time of prosperity and internal peace. It is famous for the beautiful art it produced. Carved stone statues of animals and warriors line avenues leading to the tombs of Ming Dynasty emperors.

1554 B.C.E.	Founding of the Shang Dynasty	907-959	Five Dynasties and Ten Kingdoms
1122-221 B.C.E.	Zhou Dynasty	960-1276	Song Dynasty
221-206 B.C.E.	Qin Dynasty	1276-1368	Yuan Dynasty
206 B.C.E.-220 C.E.	Han Dynasty	1368-1644	Ming Dynasty
220-581 C.E.	Wei, Jin, and Northern and Southern Dynasties	1644-1912	Qing Dynasty
		1912-1949	The Chinese Republic
581-618	Sui Dynasty	1949	The People's Republic of China
618-907	Tang Dynasty		

A Giant Emerges

North and South Korea form a peninsula 1000 km (621 mi.) long, located between Russia, China, and Japan. Much of the land is rugged and mountainous, except for a broad, fertile coastal plain that faces the Yellow Sea.

Over the centuries, ideas, inventions, and invaders from all three of its neighbors have passed through Korea. After World War II, China and the USSR struggled with the United States to gain control of the peninsula. The result was the Korean War (1950-1953). In it, United Nations forces helped the South Korean army in its fight against the North Koreans and their Chinese allies. Neither side won a clear victory. Korea was therefore divided into two separate nations — North Korea and South Korea. Efforts to reunite them began in the early 1990s.

After the war, South Korea slowly developed as an industrial power. North Korea remains virtually closed to the outside world.

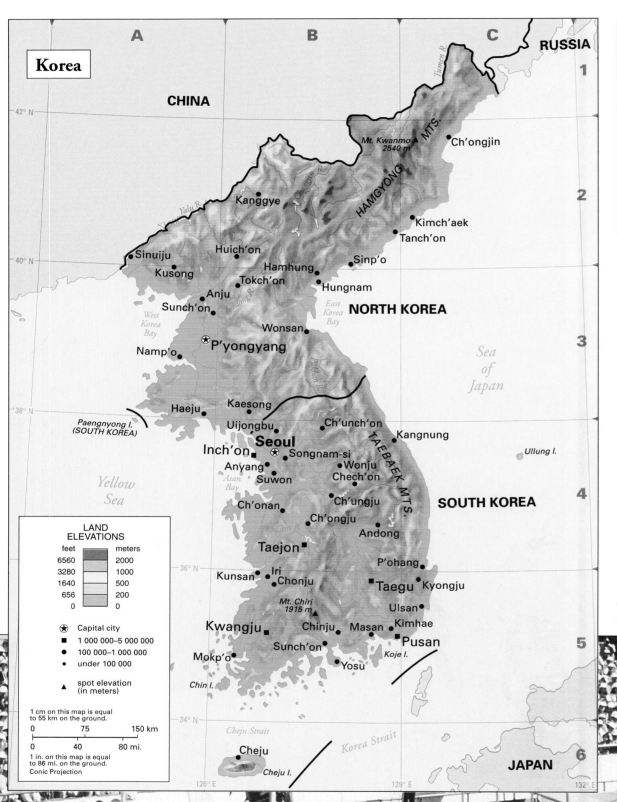

Korea

CHINA

RUSSIA

Tumen R.

Mt. Kwanmo
2540 m

Ch'ongjin

HAMGYONG MTS.

Kanggye

Kimch'aek
Tanch'on

Huich'on

Sinuiju
Kusong

Hamhung
Tokch'on

Sinp'o

Anju

Hungnam

Sunch'on

Yalu R.

West
Korea
Bay

East
Korea
Bay

NORTH KOREA

Wonsan

P'yongyang

Namp'o

Sea
of
Japan

Haeju

Kaesong

Uijongbu

Paengnyong I.
(SOUTH KOREA)

Ch'unch'on

Kangnung

Seoul
Inch'on
Songnam-si

Ullung I.

Anyang

Wonju

Suwon

Chech'on

Asan
Bay

Ch'ungju

TAEBAEK MTS.

Yellow
Sea

Ch'onan

Ch'ongju

Andong

SOUTH KOREA

Taejon

P'ohang

Kunsan
Iri
Chonju

Taegu

Kyongju

Mt. Chiri
1915 m

Ulsan

Kimhae

Kwangju

Chinju
Masan

Pusan

Sunch'on

Koje I.

Mokp'o

Yosu

Chin I.

Cheju Strait

Korea Strait

Cheju

JAPAN

Cheju I.

LAND ELEVATIONS

feet	meters
6560	2000
3280	1000
1640	500
656	200
0	0

✪ Capital city
■ 1 000 000–5 000 000
● 100 000–1 000 000
• under 100 000
▲ spot elevation (in meters)

1 cm on this map is equal to 55 km on the ground.

0   75   150 km

0   40   80 mi.

1 in. on this map is equal to 86 mi. on the ground.
Conic Projection

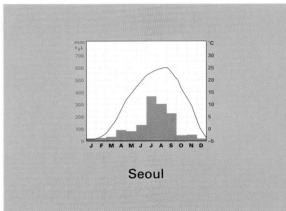

Seoul

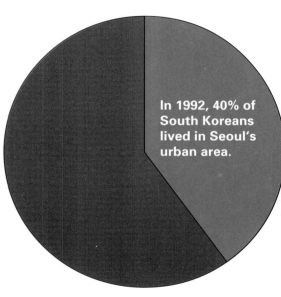

In 1992, 40% of South Koreans lived in Seoul's urban area.

The 24th Olympic Games opened in Seoul, South Korea, on September 17, 1988.

QUICK FACTS
Language: Korean
Area: 99 020 km² (38,222 sq. mi.)

Population (1994): 44 454 000
Imports (1992): US$81 405 million
Exports (1992): US$74 790 million

In 1991, textiles accounted for 27.7% of South Korea's total exports.

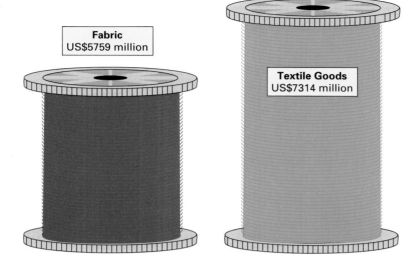

Yarn
US$976 million

Fabric
US$5759 million

Textile Goods
US$7314 million

Farming and Manufacturing

RUSSIA
CHINA
Ch'ongjin
NORTH KOREA
Hungnam
P'yongyang ✪
Wonsan
Sea of Japan
Yellow Sea
Seoul ✪
SOUTH KOREA
N
Taegu
Pusan
JAPAN
0   150 km
0   80 mi.
Conic Projection

- Rice farming
- Other farming
- Other
- Manufacturing
- Auto industry

Since 1980, South Korea has been reaching out to the world, increasing both its exports and imports.

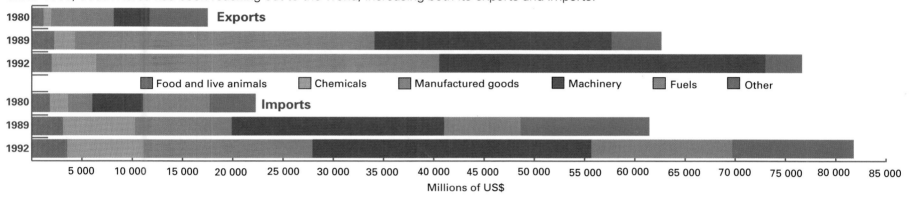

| | Food and live animals | Chemicals | Manufactured goods | Machinery | Fuels | Other |

Exports
1980
1989
1992

Imports
1980
1989
1992

5 000 10 000 15 000 20 000 25 000 30 000 35 000 40 000 45 000 50 000 55 000 60 000 65 000 70 000 75 000 80 000 85 000

Millions of US$

In the late 1980s, almost 18% of the population worked in agriculture.

Employment Distribution in South Korea

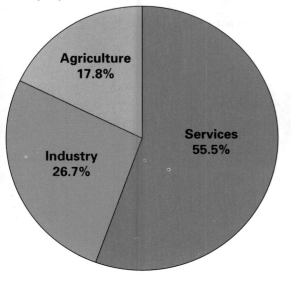

Agriculture 17.8%
Services 55.5%
Industry 26.7%

The completion of the Hyundai shipyard in 1974 marked the beginning of South Korea's growth in the shipbuilding business. The oil spill in Alaska in March, 1989, increased the world's desire for double-hulled oil tankers. This had a positive effect on the shipbuilding industry.

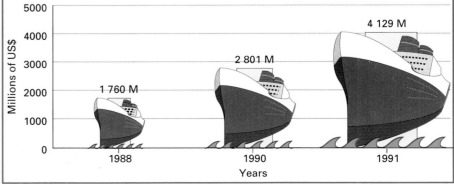

Millions of US$

5000
4000
3000
2000
1000
0

1 760 M
2 801 M
4 129 M

1988   1990   1991
Years

Exports of Newly Built Ships

An Island Nation

Japan consists of four main islands — Honshu, Hokkaido, Kyushu, and Shikoku — and thousands of smaller ones. It is a mountainous country, with many volcanoes. Due to Japan's location on the Rim of Fire, earthquakes and volcanic eruptions are major natural hazards.

Because it is so mountainous, there is little land available for farming. Also, there are few natural resources. But, it is a modern, industrial nation.

Just 150 years ago, Japan was a feudal country, closed to the outside world. Today, it has many trading partners. Yet it still has its own culture that can be traced back hundreds of years. The traditional architecture of ancient shrines and castles can be seen in many places. Traditional ceremonies still take place, and art forms such as kabuki theater are popular.

Sapporo

Kyoto

Tokyo

Miyazaki

Japan is an archipelago, made up of more than 4000 islands. It is approximately 2000 km (1242 mi.) from the northernmost tip of Hokkaido to the southern end of Kyushu. The coastline is long and, as seen here, often slopes steeply down to the sea.

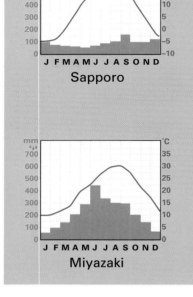

1 cm on this map is equal to 79 km on the ground

0   100   200 km

0   50   100 mi.

1 in. on this map is equal to 125 mi. on the ground
Ptolemy Simple Conic Projection

Japan

LAND ELEVATIONS

	feet	meters
	6560	2000
	3280	1000
	1640	500
	656	200
	0	0

⊛ Capital city
■ 1 000 000–5 000 000
● 100 000–1 000 000
▲ Spot elevation (in meters)

Japan is a land of great natural beauty. It has snow-capped mountains, waterfalls, forests, and beaches. There are many national parks. Tourism plays an important part in Japan's economy.

Mt. Fuji is a dormant volcano. There are many hot springs nearby that are popular bathing resorts. The mountain is considered by many Japanese to be sacred.

QUICK FACTS
Language: Japanese
Area: 377 800 km² (145,831 sq. mi.)

Population (1994): 125 023 000
Imports (1992): US$232 947 million
Exports (1992): US$339 991 million

67

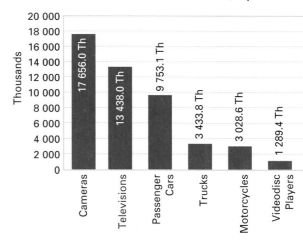

The Japanese auto industry is the largest in the world. Automakers use many robots in the manufacture of their vehicles. Still, more than five million people are employed in auto manufacturing.

Manufacturing

Electrical machinery

Transportation equipment

Metal products

General machinery

Chemicals

Ptolemy Simple Conic Projection

JAPAN

Hokkaido

Tomakomai
Muroran

Honshu

Hitachi
Tokyo
Chiba
Kawasaki
Yokohama
Yokosuka
Fuji
Toyota
Hamamatsu
Nagoya
Kyoto
Himeji
Kobe
Osaka
Sakai
Kurashiki
Hiroshima
Wakayama
Kitakyushu
Fukuoka
Oita
Shikoku

Kyushu

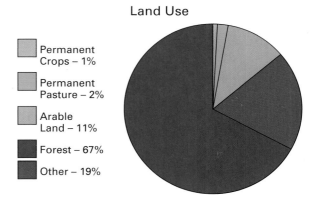

Selected Products Manufactured, by Units

Thousands

Cameras	17 656.0 Th
Televisions	13 438.0 Th
Passenger Cars	9 753.1 Th
Trucks	3 433.8 Th
Motorcycles	3 028.6 Th
Videodisc Players	1 289.4 Th

Land Use

- Permanent Crops – 1%
- Permanent Pasture – 2%
- Arable Land – 11%
- Forest – 67%
- Other – 19%

Many farmers use modern methods and technology to help produce greater yields. Traditional rice fields are now often harvested by computerized combines.

Because Japan is so mountainous, space for living and for farming is very valuable. Most of it is found in short, narrow, river valleys and on a few small plains. One of the most important of these is the Kanto Plain.

JAPAN

Hokkaido

Honshu

Shikoku

Kyushu

Land Use

- Rice
- Other grains
- Horticulture and orchards
- Mulberry fields (silk)
- Forest
- Urban regions

Ptolemy Simple Conic Projection

There is a limited amount of level land available for farming. Japanese farmers have made good use of terracing in order to grow more crops. Rice, vegetables, tree fruits, and other crops are cultivated in terraces like these.

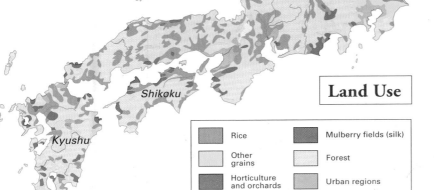

"Land of the Rising Sun"

Archaeologists believe that the ancestors of today's Japanese arrived on the islands about 2000 years ago. They came from mainland Asia, and brought with them the techniques for growing rice, as well as for making bronze.

Japan's physical isolation has greatly affected its culture and history. The Heian period (794 –1190 C.E.) was a golden age for Japanese nobles. Art, music, and literature flourished. This era in Japan's history came to an end when the samurai warriors took control of the country. After a fierce civil war between two samurai clans, the winner, Minamoto Yoritomo, set up his own government and capital city in Kamakura. He took the title of shogun, which means "barbarian-quelling-great-general". There was still an emperor, but he was virtually powerless.

The centuries after this are sometimes called Japan's Dark Ages, in which feudal lords warred for power and territory. At the end of this, the country was again unified by a powerful shogun. The shoguns then kept the country under military rule. They did not allow trade or communication with the rest of the world. Japan was isolated and closed to outsiders.

This ended in 1853, when US Commodore Matthew Perry's "black ships" (so-called because they were powered by steam) sailed into Tokyo Bay. The following year, Japan and the United States signed a trade agreement. A few years later, with power restored to the emperor, the Meiji Reforms began the rapid modernization of Japan.

Ikebana, the art of formal flower arranging, began with the use of flowers to decorate statues of Buddha. For many years, men, including samurai warriors, took part in competitions held at Buddhist festivals. Only in recent times have women practiced ikebana.

Tea was brought to Japan from China by Buddhist monks in the 8th century C.E. For a long time, it was very hard to obtain and was considered a luxury. Ceremonies were created around the serving and drinking of tea. The chanoyu, or tea ceremony, is still held today.

Woodblock printing is one of the best known forms of Japanese art. During the 19th century, prints such as this one were very popular among western art collectors.

Ancient Divisions and Provinces Before 1865

Legend:
- Shrine or temple
- Provincial boundaries

N

JAPAN

DEWA
MUTSU
SADO
SALO
Hondo (Honshu)
NOTO
ECHIGO
KAGA
ETCHU
SHIMOTSUKE
HIDA
SHINANO
KOZUKE
HITACHI
WAKASA
YAMASHIRO
TANGO
ECHIZEN
MUSASHI
TAJIMA
MINO
KAI
SHIMOSA
MIMASAKA
INABA
OKI
HOKI
TAMBA
OMI
KAZUSA
IZUMO
MIKAWA
SURUGA
IWAMI
BINGO
HARIMA
ISE
IZU
AWA
TSUSHIMA
AKI
BIZEN
SETTSU
TOTOMI
SAGAMI
NAGATO
SUO
BITCHU
SANUKI
AWAJI
OWARI
YAMATO
IGA
CHIKUZEN
IKI
BUZEN
IYO
TOSA
AWA
IZUMI
KII
HIZEN
SHIMA
HIGO
BUNGO
KAWACHI
CHIKUGO
SATSUMA
HYUGA
OSUMI

Shikoku

Kyushu

Ptolemy Simple Conic Projection

During the Edo Period, Japan had two capital cities. The shoguns ruled from the city of Edo (present-day Tokyo), while the emperor — who by this time was powerless — remained in Kyoto. Tokugawa Ieyasu (1542-1616) was the first shogun of this period. His family ruled Japan for the next 250 years, not permitting any trade or communication with the rest of the world.

The Tokugawa shoguns made the daimyos, or lords, follow a policy known as sankin kotai, or alternate attendance. Every second year, the daimyo had to pack up all his possessions and move from his home yashiki (castle) to his yashiki in the capital city of Edo.

Ezo (Hokkaido)

Hakodate
Matsumae
Noshiro
Miyako
Sakata
JAPAN
Niigata
Shiroishi
N
Hondo (Honshu)
Sabae
Edo (Tokyo)
Usaka (Osaka)
Nakasendo
Sumpu (Shizuoka)
Uraga
Kanagawa (Kamakura)
Kyoto
Fushimi
Hyogo
Shimoda
Yamaguchi
Shikoku
Arima
Nagasaki
Kyushu

Ptolemy Simple Conic Projection

The Edo Period: 1600–1860

Legend	
Castle towns	Lands controlled by Shogun's supporters
Shogun's lands	Lands controlled by Dependents
Lands controlled by Shogun's relatives	Major travel and transport routes

QUICK FACTS   Only samurai were allowed to wear two swords.
The world's first novel written by a woman was published in the Heian period.
"Japan" comes from the Chinese word "Jih-pen", meaning "the source of the sun".

69

Zen Buddhism was introduced into Japan from China. It stressed simplicity, discipline, and a fearless attitude toward death. Zen became the religion of the samurai.

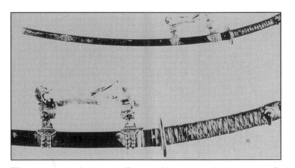

The samurai were allowed to wear two swords. Both were razor sharp, and could cut off an opponent's head with one slash. The swords were made by elite, master craftsmen.

The samurai lived according to the code of bushido, which means the way of the warrior. Bushido stresses discipline, loyalty, and obedience. A samurai would commit suicide if his lord ordered him to do so.

Timeline

30 000 B.C.E.	PREHISTORY
10 000–300 B.C.E.	*Jomon period* 660 B.C.E. Emperor Jimmu comes down to earth in a stone boat.
300 B.C.E.–300 C.E.	*Yayoi period* 300 C.E. Rise of the Yamato clan
500–1190	THE AGE OF EMPERORS 587 Soga victory and the introduction of Buddhism to Japan 710 First permanent capital city built in Nara 794 Capital moved to Kyoto
794–1190	*Heian period* 1010 "The Tale of Genji" is written.
1190–1600	THE MEDIEVAL PERIOD 1192 Minamoto Yoritomo, the first shogun, sets up his bakufu in Kamakura. 1540 The Portuguese arrive.
1600–1860	THE EDO PERIOD 1600 Tokugawa Ieyasu takes control of Japan and sets up his bakufu in Edo. 1853 Arrival of Commodore Perry's "black ships"
1860–1890	THE MEIJI REFORM PERIOD 1868 Meiji reforms and the return of formal power to the emperors
1890–1945	THE AGE OF IMPERIALISM 1926 Hirohito becomes emperor

Himeji Castle, on the island of Honshu, is regarded as the most beautiful castle in Japan. It was built in the 16th century as the seat of a daimyo — a feudal lord who gave allegiance to the shogun.

City Life

More than 77% percent of Japan's 125 million people live in cities. It is expected that by the year 2000, Tokyo and its surrounding area will still have the highest urban population in the world. Almost all of Japan's major cities are ports, located on the small, scattered lowlands along the coasts of this island nation. The shortage of level land means that these cities are densely populated, and every square meter of space is used as carefully as possible.

Since Japan is highly dependent on imported raw materials and export markets for its finished products, most large factories are located on the waterfronts of port cities such as Tokyo/Yokohama, Osaka/Kobe, Nagoya, and Kitakyushu. Because level land is so scarce, many of these industries are built on land reclaimed from the sea.

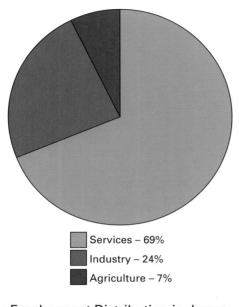

- Services – 69%
- Industry – 24%
- Agriculture – 7%

Employment Distribution in Japan

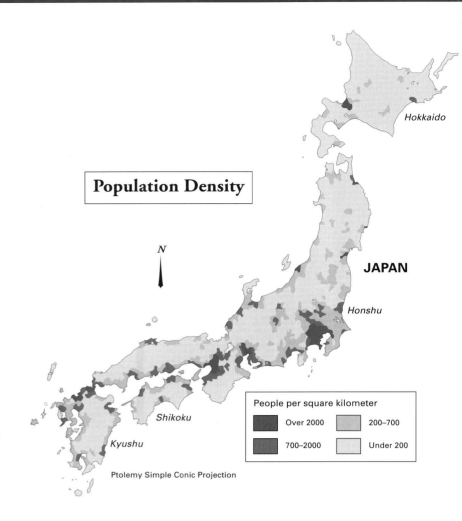

Population Density

N

JAPAN

Hokkaido

Honshu

Shikoku

Kyushu

People per square kilometer

Over 2000	200–700
700–2000	Under 200

Ptolemy Simple Conic Projection

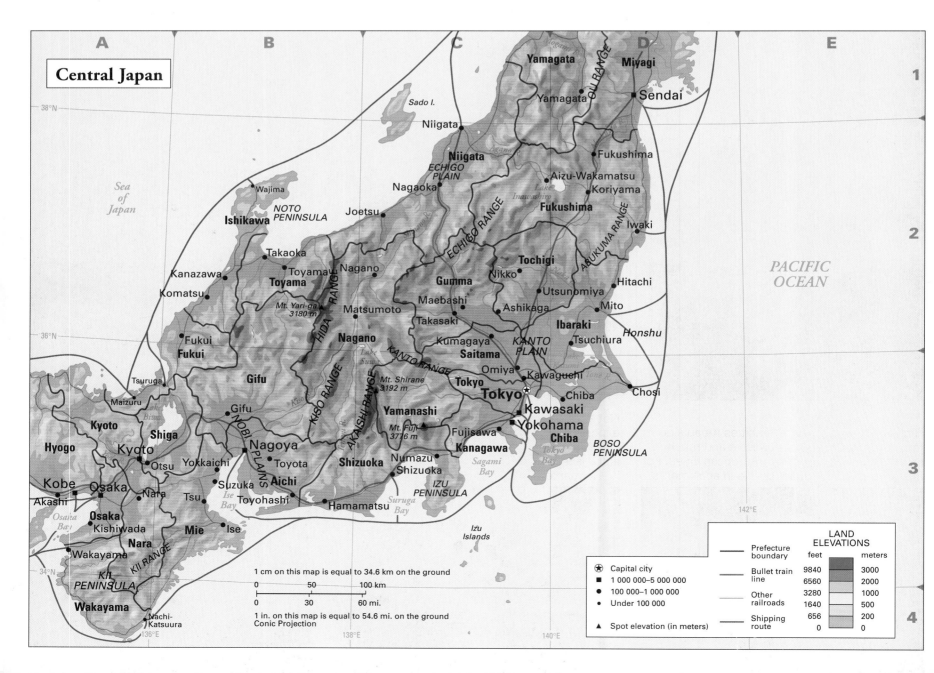

Central Japan

Sea of Japan

PACIFIC OCEAN

Yamagata • Miyagi
Yamagata • Sendai

Sado I.

Niigata
Fukushima
Niigata
ECHIGO PLAIN
Nagaoka
Aizu-Wakamatsu
Koriyama
Wajima
NOTO PENINSULA
Joetsu
Fukushima
Iwaki
Ishikawa
ECHIGO RANGE
ABUKUMA RANGE
Takaoka
Nagano
Tochigi
Hitachi
Kanazawa
Toyama
Toyama
Gumma
Nikko
Komatsu
HIDA RANGE
Matsumoto
Maebashi
Utsunomiya
Ashikaga
Mito
Mt. Yari-ga 3180 m
Takasaki
Honshu
Fukui
Nagano
Kumagaya
Ibaraki
Tsuchiura
Fukui
KANTO RANGE
Saitama
KANTO PLAIN
Gifu
KISO RANGE
Mt. Shirane 3192 m
Omiya
Kawaguchi
Tsuruga
AKAISHI RANGE
Tokyo
Tokyo
Chosi
Maizuru
Gifu
Yamanashi
Chiba
Kyoto
NOBI PLAINS
Mt. Fuji 3776 m
Kawasaki
Shiga
Nagoya
Fujisawa
Yokohama
Hyogo
Kyoto
Aichi
Shizuoka
Kanagawa
Chiba
Otsu
Yokkaichi
Toyota
Numazu
BOSO PENINSULA
Kobe
Osaka
Suzuka
Shizuoka
Shizuoka
Tokyo Bay
Akashi
Nara
Tsu
Toyohashi
Mie
Ise
Hamamatsu
Sagami Bay
Osaka Bay
Osaka
IZU PENINSULA
Kishiwada
Suruga Bay
Nara
Izu Islands
Wakayama
KII RANGE
KII PENINSULA
Wakayama
Nachi-Katsuura

1 cm on this map is equal to 34.6 km on the ground

0   50   100 km
0   30   60 mi.

1 in. on this map is equal to 54.6 mi. on the ground
Conic Projection

⊛ Capital city
■ 1 000 000–5 000 000
● 100 000–1 000 000
• Under 100 000
▲ Spot elevation (in meters)

Prefecture boundary
Bullet train line
Other railroads
Shipping route

LAND ELEVATIONS

feet	meters
9840	3000
6560	2000
3280	1000
1640	500
656	200
0	0

QUICK FACTS
Population density of Japan: 330.9 people/km² (857/sq. mi.)
Area of Japan: 377 800 km² (145,830 sq. mi.)

Population density of Tokyo: 10 086 people/km² (26,122/sq. mi.)
Area of Tokyo: 2821 km² (1089 sq. mi.)

71

Tokyo

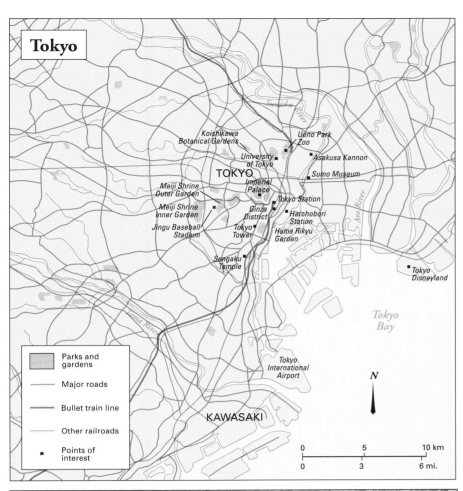

Koishikawa Botanical Gardens
Ueno Park Zoo
University of Tokyo
Asakusa Kannon
TOKYO
Sumo Museum
Meiji Shrine Outer Garden
Imperial Palace
Tokyo Station
Meiji Shrine Inner Garden
Ginza District
Hatchobori Station
Jingu Baseball Stadium
Tokyo Tower
Hama Rikyu Garden
Sengaku Temple
Tokyo Disneyland

Ara River
Sumida River
Tama River

Tokyo Bay
Tokyo International Airport

KAWASAKI

N

Parks and gardens
Major roads
Bullet train line
Other railroads
Points of interest

0   5   10 km
0   3   6 mi.

The Imperial Palace is the home of Japan's emperor. The building occupies almost 25 ha (62 acres) in the heart of Tokyo. Because of the high value of land in the city, the palace is said to be one of the world's most expensive pieces of real estate.

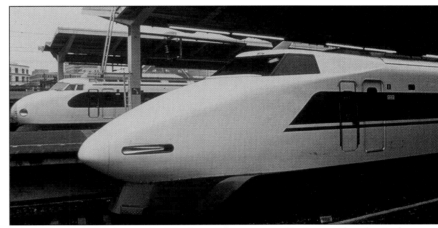

It can sometimes be as fast to travel from one city to another by train as by air. The high-speed Shinkansen, or bullet train, travels at speeds of more than 200 km/h (124 mph). They were once the fastest trains in the world. Today, though, the French TGV system holds that title.

Tokyo has the highest population of any city in the world.

Tingo Baseball Ground

Baseball is a popular sport in Japan. Use of land for recreation or sports is rare, because it is expensive. Golf courses have been created in the basements of large office buildings. Tennis courts are often built on rooftops.

The Ginza is Tokyo's most popular shopping and entertainment center. The goods sold here are expensive, because rents and taxes on this valuable land are very high.

High land costs in Japanese cities mean single-family homes are very expensive and much smaller than those in North American cities. For this reason, most Japanese live in apartments.

Not all of the cars produced in Japan are exported. But growing traffic congestion in the cities and high fuel prices have made automakers produce much smaller cars for their home market. These are known as "city cars".

Nakamise Street in the Asakusa district of Tokyo is a popular shopping area that has been covered to protect pedestrians from the hot, rainy weather of summer and the cool, damp weather of winter.

The World's Largest Nation

With an area of more than 17 million km² (6.5 million sq. mi.), Russia is the largest country on earth, and spans two continents, Europe and Asia. Russia's Pacific coastline stretches from the Bering Sea to the Sea of Japan.

Asiatic Russia, often called Siberia, is a huge, sparsely populated land area, about the size of China. More than 50% of the mountains, hills, and plains in this region are covered in coniferous and mixed forests. The largest area of level land is the West Siberian Plain, located between the Ural Mountains and the Yenisey River. East of the Yenisey, the landscape is one of rugged plateaus and mountain ranges. The Kamchatka Peninsula lies along the edge of the Pacific Plate, and there are 120 volcanoes in this area, 23 of which are currently active. The highest, Klyuchevskaya Sopka, is 4750 m (15,590 ft).

Siberia is rich in minerals, fossil fuels, and forests. Due to its isolation from the rest of the country, the vast distances involved, and the harsh climate, many of these natural resources are still undeveloped. Some of the resource-poor countries of Asia, such as Japan, are investing money to help Russia tap these resources.

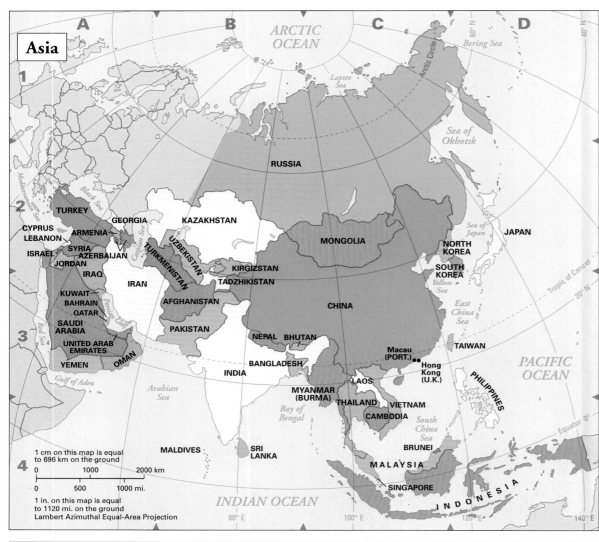

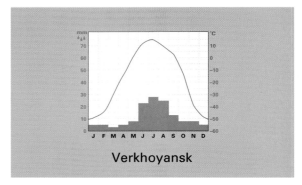

Verkhoyansk

As well as being the main Russian naval base in Asia, Vladisvostok is an important seaport for Russian imports of grain from Canada and the United States.

QUICK FACTS
Area: 17 075 000 km² (6,590,950 sq. mi.)
Approximately 20% of Russia's population lives in Asiatic Russia.

Nearly 75% of Russia's land mass lies in Asia.
The port at Vladivostok is kept open in winter by ice-breaker ships.

73

The Karymsky volcano is only one of the many that are located on the Kamchatka Peninsula.

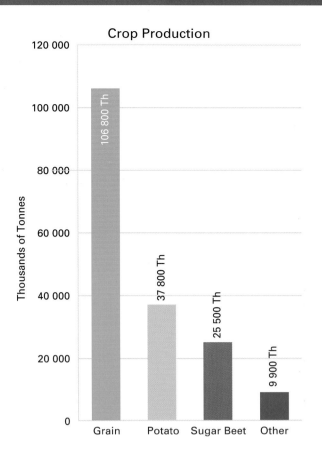

Crop Production

Thousands of Tonnes

- Grain: 106 800 Th
- Potato: 37 800 Th
- Sugar Beet: 25 500 Th
- Other: 9 900 Th

Much of Asiatic Russia is sparsely populated. The land is rugged and the slopes are forest-covered in many areas.

Land Use in Russia

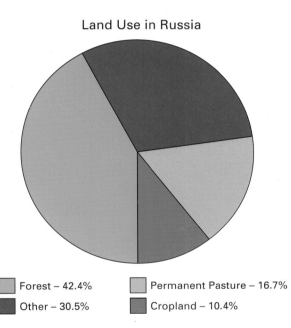

- Forest – 42.4%
- Permanent Pasture – 16.7%
- Other – 30.5%
- Cropland – 10.4%

Coal is one of many natural resources found in Siberia.

For many years, Asiatic Russia was isolated from the rest of the country. Construction of the Trans-Siberian Railway began in 1891 and continued, as it was gradually expanded, until 1917. The railroad runs from Yekaterinburg, all the way to Vladivostok.

A Nation Built on Trade

Canada is the second largest country in the world by area. Its population, however, is quite low, giving Canada one of the lowest population densities in the world.

Rich in natural resources, Canada is an important trading nation, exporting products worldwide from the country's forests, mines, farms, and fisheries. Japan imports coal and wood products from British Columbia. China and Russia are major customers for Canadian grain from the prairie provinces.

Manufactured goods also play an important role in Canada's trade with the rest of the world. Industrial equipment, machinery, and automobiles and related products account for a large part of Canada's exports and imports. Telecommunications equipment and rapid transit systems are designed and built in many urban centers across the country.

Since the 19th century, Vancouver has been Canada's gateway to the Pacific. It is a busy seaport, and one of the fastest-growing cities in North America.

Population Change in British Columbia and in Canada, 1976-1991

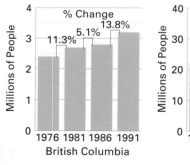

British Columbia — Millions of People
% Change
11.3%   5.1%   13.8%
1976 1981 1986 1991

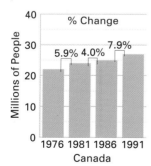

Canada — Millions of People
% Change
5.9%   4.0%   7.9%
1976 1981 1986 1991

Canada

- ✪ Capital city
- ★ Provincial or territorial capital
- ■ 1 000 000–5 000 000
- ● 100 000–1 000 000
- • Under 100 000

ARCTIC OCEAN

Alaska (U.S.)

Yukon Territory

Dawson

★ Whitehorse

Inuvik

Beaufort Sea

Banks Island

Prince of Wales I.

Victoria Island

Great Bear Lake

Northwest Territories

Baker Lake

★ Yellowknife

Great Slave Lake

Lake Athabasca

Reindeer Lake

Churchill

Heiberg I.

Devon I.

Ellesme

Magnetic North Pole +

British Columbia

Prince Rupert

Kitimat

Queen Charlotte Is.

Prince George

Dawson Creek

Grande-Prairie

Fort McMurray

Alberta

Saskatchewan

Manitoba

Thompson

Edmonton ★

Red Deer

North Battleford

Prince Albert

Saskatoon

Lake Winnipeg

Vancouver Island

Kamloops

Calgary

Nanaimo

Vancouver

Kelowna

Lake Winnipegosis

Victoria ★

Nelson

Medicine Hat

Swift Current

Moose Jaw

★ Regina

Lake Manitoba

Portage la Prairie

Kenora

PACIFIC OCEAN

Trail

Lethbridge

Brandon

Winnipeg ★

Lake of the Woods

UNITED STATES

Canada is one of the world's leading wheat exporters. Wheat from Saskatchewan is shipped by rail to ports such as Vancouver and Prince Rupert, where it is loaded for export to Pacific Rim countries.

QUICK FACTS
Languages: English and French
Area: 9 916 140 km² (3,828,625 sq. mi.)

Population (1994): 29 100 000
Imports (1992): US$127 951 million
Exports (1992): US$133 447 million

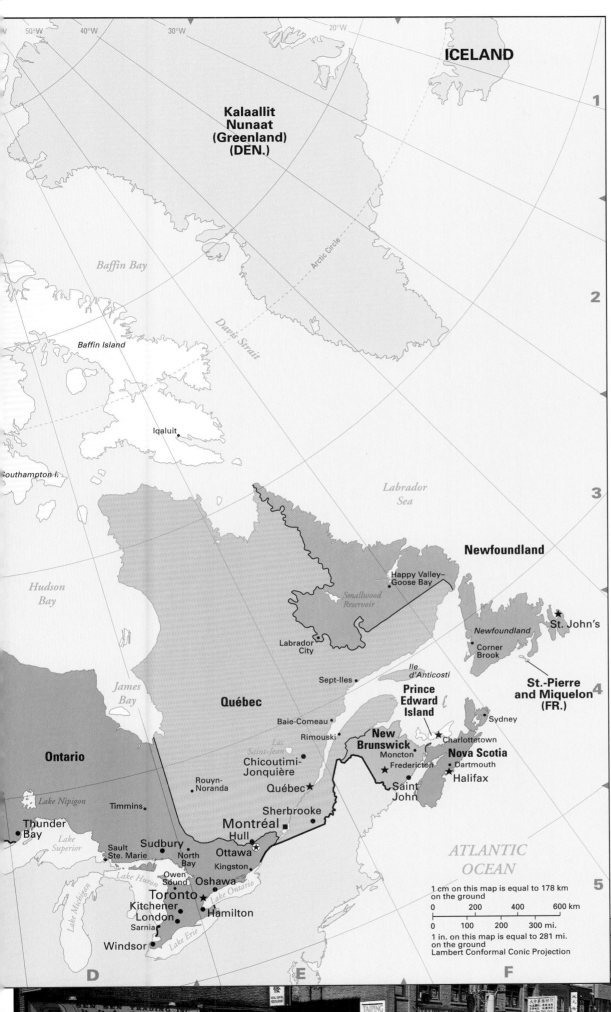

Alberta has vast oil deposits, and is a major supplier of petroleum products for domestic use and for export to the United States.

Types of Imports and Exports

Imports

- Forest Products – 1%
- Energy – 5%
- Agriculture & Fish Products – 6%
- Other Consumer Goods – 11%
- Industrial Goods & Materials – 20%
- Automobile Products – 24%
- Machinery & Equipment – 33%

Exports

- Other Consumer Goods – 2%
- Agriculture & Fish Products – 8%
- Energy – 9%
- Forest Products – 16%
- Machinery & Equipment – 18%
- Industrial Goods & Materials – 22%
- Automobile Products – 25%

Toronto, the capital city of Ontario, is Canada's largest and most cosmopolitan city, with a population of approximately four million.

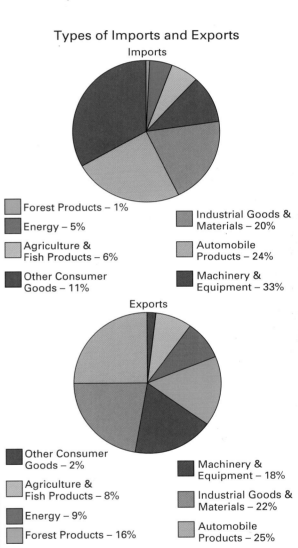

Canada's Pacific Province

British Columbia, Canada's gateway to the Pacific, is the most westerly province in the country.

There are many different environments in British Columbia, ranging from desert to rainforest, and from plains to mountains. Winter temperatures vary greatly across the province. Coastal areas seldom see the thermometer fall to less than 0°C (32°F), while temperatures in the interior can fall to well below – 40°C (– 40°F). Summers are generally temperate throughout the province, with temperatures between 15°C (59°F) and 30°C (86°F). As much as 3000 mm (117 in.) of precipitation can fall annually on the western slopes of the Coast Mountains. The Okanagan Valley might receive as little as 250 mm (10 in.).

Much of the trade and other contact between Canada and the nations of Asia is funneled through the ports and cities of coastal British Columbia. Of these, Vancouver is the most important. The Port of Vancouver handles the importing and exporting of raw materials such as wheat, lumber, paper, coal, oil, and sulfur, as well as finished products such as automobiles, machinery, and other manufactured goods. Vancouver's airport is a major departure and arrival point for tourists, business people, and government officials heading to or coming from Japan, Hong Kong, Singapore, and all the other nations of the Pacific Rim.

At 3954 m (12,972 ft.), Mount Robson is the highest mountain in the Canadian Rockies. The magnificent mountains in British Columbia and the superb skiing they offer are a major attraction for travelers from Japan and elsewhere in the Pacific Rim. Tourism is one of the fastest-growing industries in the world.

Only 3% of the land in British Columbia is suitable for agriculture. Of this land, 90% is in the Fort St. John region.

Vancouver is Canada's gateway to the Pacific. The majority of flights from Canada to the countries of the Pacific and Asia pass through this busy airport. Modern telecommunications and air travel mean that the huge Pacific Ocean is no longer the barrier it once was.

Approximately 50% of British Columbia is forest-covered. The heavy precipitation and long growing season are ideal for rainforests. Forestry is a major, although sometimes controversial, industry in British Columbia.

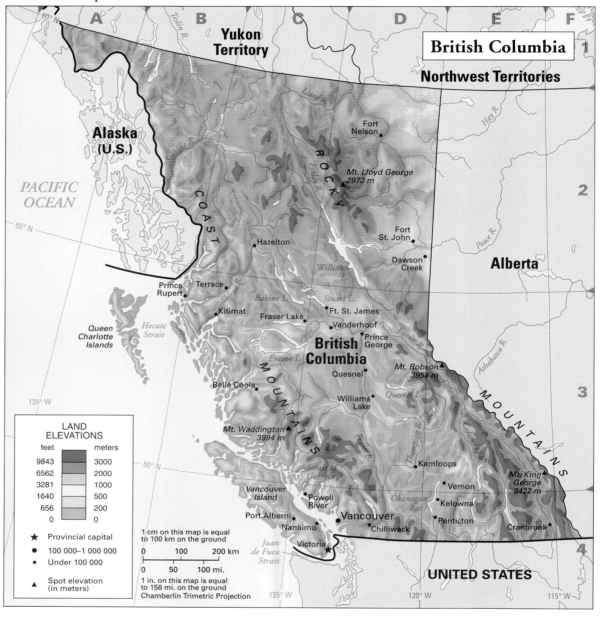

British Columbia

LAND ELEVATIONS

feet	meters
9843	3000
6562	2000
3281	1000
1640	500
656	200
0	0

★ Provincial capital
● 100 000–1 000 000
• Under 100 000
▲ Spot elevation (in meters)

1 cm on this map is equal to 100 km on the ground

1 in. on this map is equal to 158 mi. on the ground
Chamberlin Trimetric Projection

The city of Vancouver is the hub around which much of Canada's trade with its Pacific partners revolves. British Columbia is one of the most urbanized provinces in Canada.

QUICK FACTS Area: 948 601 km² (366,255 sq. mi.)
Population (1991): 3 282 061
British Columbia joined Canadian Confederation in 1871.

77

Historical British Columbia

British Columbia's attraction to traders and adventurers was twofold. First was the search for the northwest passage — a direct route from Europe across the Atlantic to the riches of "the East". Second was the dream of instant wealth from British Columbia's fur, gold, silver, and other natural resources.

Europeans and Canadians of note who traveled the coast or interior of British Columbia included the Spaniard Don Juan Pérez, the British Captains James Cook and George Vancouver, and Simon Fraser, a partner in the North West Company.

Trade was already well-established among the Native peoples when Europeans arrived in the province. Goods traveled from the coast to the interior along "grease trails", so-called because of the oil that was carried over them. The Natives' trading involvement with Canadians and Europeans was an important part of the settlement and development of the British Columbia of today.

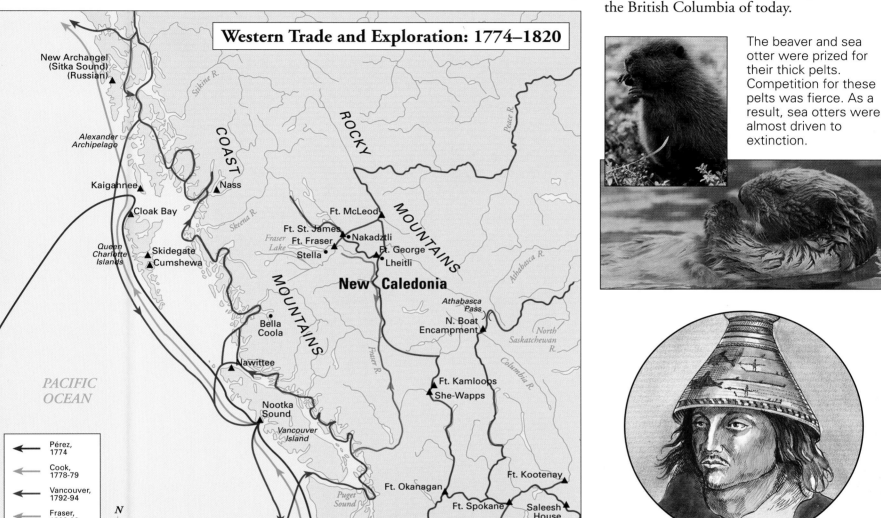

Western Trade and Exploration: 1774–1820

New Archangel (Sitka Sound) (Russian)

Alexander Archipelago

Kaigahnee

Cloak Bay

Queen Charlotte Islands

Skidegate
Cumshewa

PACIFIC OCEAN

Nass

Skeena R.

COAST MOUNTAINS

Ft. McLeod

Ft. St. James
Fraser Lake Ft. Fraser • Nakadztli
Stella • Ft. George
• Lheitli

New Caledonia

ROCKY MOUNTAINS

Peace R.

Athabasca R.

Athabasca Pass
N. Boat Encampment

North Saskatchewan R.

Columbia R.

Bella Coola

Nawittee

Fraser R.

MOUNTAINS

Nootka Sound

Vancouver Island

Ft. Kamloops
She-Wapps

Ft. Okanagan

Puget Sound

Ft. Spokane

Ft. Kootenay

Saleesh House

Ft. Clatsop
Astoria (Ft. George)

Snake R.

Columbia R.

Ft. Nez Percé (Ft. Walla Walla)

Pérez, 1774
Cook, 1778-79
Vancouver, 1792-94
Fraser, 1806-09
Trading route
▲ Trading post
• Native community

N

0   100   200 km
0 50 100 mi.
Chamberlin Trimetric Projection

The beaver and sea otter were prized for their thick pelts. Competition for these pelts was fierce. As a result, sea otters were almost driven to extinction.

Chief Maquinna (?-1795) Maquinna was one of the leaders of the Nuucha-nulth (Nootka) people, who controlled much of the coastal fur trade in the late 18th century. He is thought to have met Captain James Cook and certainly did meet and aid Captain George Vancouver, after whom the city and island of Vancouver are named.

In this copy of a painting by C.W. Jefferys, newly arrived Europeans are greeted by Native peoples. In this way, trading relationships were established.

Simon Fraser (1776-1852) Fraser was the first European to navigate what is now called the Fraser River to the Pacific coast, shooting dangerous rapids on the way. He was also responsible for setting up early fur-trading posts in British Columbia's interior.

The World's Largest Trader

The United States trades more with other nations than does any other country in the world. Each year, the USA exports more than US$440 billion worth of goods to other countries, including Canada, Japan, Mexico and Taiwan.

As well, the United States is the fourth largest country in the world in terms of area and has the third largest population.

Alaska, Washington, Oregon, California, and Hawaii are the Pacific Rim States.

Hawaii became a possession of the United States in 1898, and the 50th State in 1959. Tourism, tropical fruits such as pineapples, and the large military bases in the islands are all important to the Hawaiian economy.

San Francisco is a major port as well as an important center of finance and international trade. Its cosmopolitan population comes from many areas of the Pacific Rim.

United States

Honolulu ★ **Hawaii**

1 cm on this map is equal to 141 km on the ground
0   100   200 km
0   100 mi.
1 in. on this map is equal to 222 mi. on the ground
Albers Equal-Area Projection

1 cm on this map is equal to 318 km on the ground
0   400   800 km
0   400 mi.
1 in. on this map is equal to 503 mi. on the ground
Albers Equal-Area Projection

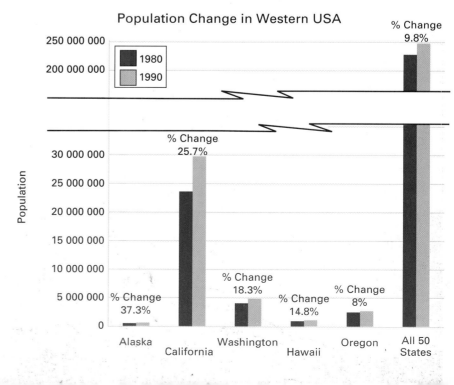

Population Change in Western USA

- 1980
- 1990

% Change 9.8%

% Change 25.7%

% Change 37.3%

% Change 18.3%

% Change 14.8%

% Change 8%

Population

250 000 000
200 000 000
30 000 000
25 000 000
20 000 000
15 000 000
10 000 000
5 000 000
0

Alaska   California   Washington   Hawaii   Oregon   All 50 States

QUICK FACTS
Language: English
Area: 9 372 610 km² (3,617,827 sq. mi.)

Population (1994): 260 750 000
Imports (1992): US$552 616 million
Exports (1992): US$447 400 million

Map labels:

CANADA

Maine
Minnesota · Duluth · Fargo
Minneapolis · St. Paul
Wisconsin · Milwaukee · Madison
Iowa · Des Moines
Sioux Falls
Omaha · Lincoln
Michigan · Lansing · Detroit
Lake Superior · Lake Huron · Lake Michigan · Lake Erie · Lake Ontario
Chicago · Gary · Toledo · Cleveland
Illinois · Indiana · Ohio · Columbus · Wheeling
Springfield · Indianapolis · Cincinnati
Topeka · Kansas City · St. Louis
Jefferson City · Missouri
Wichita · Louisville · Frankfort · Charleston · 4.
Kentucky · Virginia · Richmond
Oklahoma · Oklahoma City
Arkansas · Little Rock · Memphis
Tennessee · Knoxville · Nashville
North Carolina · Raleigh · Charlotte
Dallas · Fort Worth
Birmingham · Alabama · Mississippi · Jackson · Montgomery
Georgia · Atlanta · Columbia
South Carolina · Charleston
Louisiana · Baton Rouge · New Orleans · Mobile
Houston
Gulf of Mexico
Jacksonville · Tallahassee
Florida · Tampa · Miami
Burlington · Montpelier · 2. · Augusta · Portland
Manchester · 1. · Concord · Boston
Albany · New York · 3. · Providence · Hartford
Buffalo · Rhode Island · Connecticut
Pennsylvania · Newark · New York
Harrisburg · Pittsburgh · Trenton · New Jersey
Baltimore · Philadelphia · Dover
Annapolis · Delaware · Maryland
Washington, D.C.
ATLANTIC OCEAN
BAHAMAS
CUBA

1 cm on this map is equal to 160 km on the ground
0 | 200 | 400 | 600 km
0 | 100 | 200 | 300 mi.
1 in. on this map is equal to 253 mi. on the ground
Albers Equal-Area Projection

National capital
State capital
■ Over 5 000 000
■ 1 000 000–5 000 000
● 100 000–1 000 000
· Under 100 000

1. Vermont
2. New Hampshire
3. Massachusetts
4. West Virginia

United States Trade with Selected Countries		
	Imports from	Exports to
Australia	—	2.0%
Canada	17.8%	20.2%
China	3.4%	1.7%
Hong Kong	1.8%	2.0%
Indonesia	0.8%	—
Japan	17.6%	10.7%
Malaysia	1.5%	1.0%
Mexico	6.4%	9.1%
Philippines	0.8%	0.6%
Taiwan	4.2%	3.4%
Other	45.7%	49.3%

Alaska, the most northerly state, has enormous natural resources. The Trans-Alaska pipeline carries crude petroleum approximately 1300 km (800 mi.) from the oilfields of Prudhoe Bay to the Pacific port of Valdez.

Seattle is one of the major ports of the northwest region of the USA. The city has a mild climate, attractive setting, and high standard of living. It is a leading center of aircraft manufacture, aerospace research, and computer software development.

The economy of Oregon is based on forestry and agriculture. Portland is its largest city and port.

"...to Shining Sea"

In general, the west coast of the United States has cooler summers and warmer winters than the rest of the country. This is due to the waters of the Pacific Ocean that modify temperatures, cooling the air in summer and warming it in winter. The Alaska Current carries warmer water to the coast of Washington State, while the cold California Current affects California and Mexico.

Vegetation and climate are closely linked. All along this coast, heavy rainfall and mild temperatures promote the growth of large evergreen trees such as the sequoia, or giant redwood, the Douglas fir, and western red cedar. Further inland the trees are smaller because they receive less precipitation.

To the south, in southern California, Nevada, and Arizona, the climate is very dry. The cactus is a common plant here. In the dry interior, areas of forest are found on the slopes of high mountains, where air is forced to rise, then drops enough precipitation to support the growth of evergreen trees.

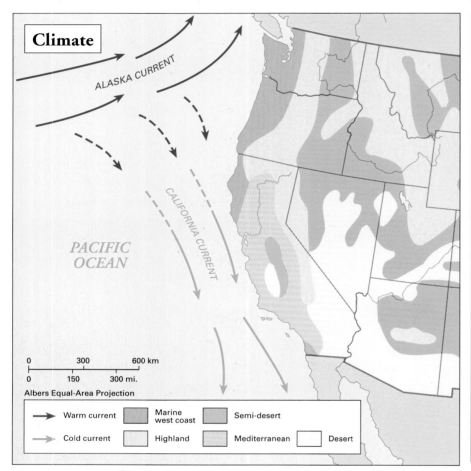

Because of variations in climate due to altitude, it is possible to sail and ski in the same day in Washington State.

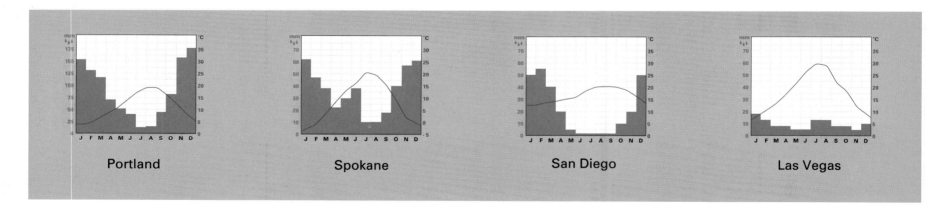

Portland

Spokane

San Diego

Las Vegas

Vegetation Types: Cross section #1; Olympic Peninsula, Washington to Denver, Colorado

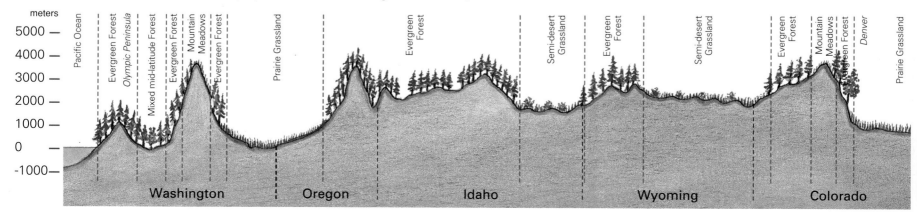

QUICK FACTS The world's tallest tree, a California redwood, is 110 m (362 ft.) high.
The oldest living things on earth, Bristlecone pines in the Inyo National Forest, California, are thought to be 4700 years old.
The highest temperature ever recorded in the United States was 57°C (134°F) at Death Valley, California, in 1913.

81

Population Density

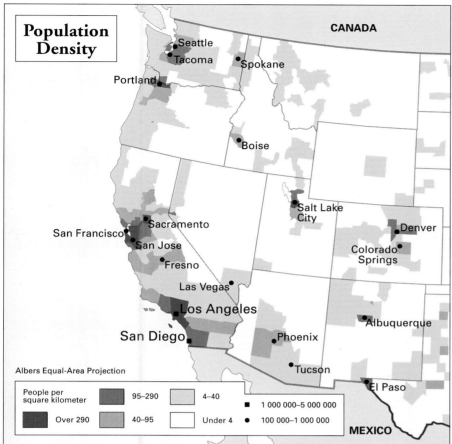

Albers Equal-Area Projection

People per square kilometer			
Over 290	95–290	4–40	■ 1 000 000–5 000 000
	40–95	Under 4	● 100 000–1 000 000

Map labels: CANADA, Seattle, Tacoma, Spokane, Portland, Boise, Salt Lake City, Denver, Colorado Springs, San Francisco, Sacramento, San Jose, Fresno, Las Vegas, Los Angeles, San Diego, Phoenix, Albuquerque, Tucson, El Paso, MEXICO

Vegetation

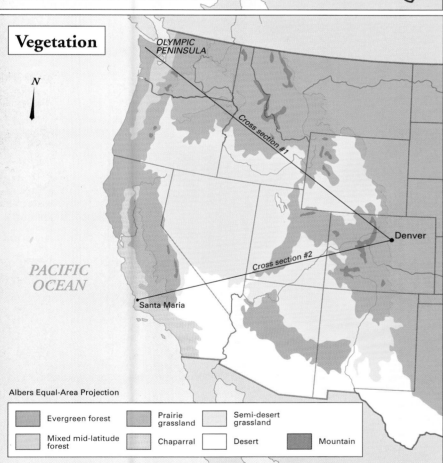

N

OLYMPIC PENINSULA

Cross section #1

Cross section #2

Denver

Santa Maria

PACIFIC OCEAN

Albers Equal-Area Projection

Evergreen forest	Prairie grassland	Semi-desert grassland
Mixed mid-latitude forest	Chaparral	Desert
		Mountain

The Joshua Tree National Monument in California is a good example of the type of desert found on the eastern side of the mountains.

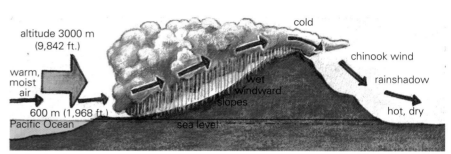

altitude 3000 m (9,842 ft.)

cold

chinook wind

warm, moist air

rainshadow

Wet windward slopes

hot, dry

600 m (1,968 ft.)

Pacific Ocean

sea level

Rainshadow Areas Westerly winds blowing off the Pacific bring moist air. As the air is forced over the mountains, it cools, clouds form, and the moisture is released. The drier areas on the eastern side of the mountains are called "rainshadows".

These California redwood trees thrive in the heavy rainfall and mild temperatures along the Pacific coast.

Vegetation Types: Cross section #2; Santa Maria, California to Denver, Colorado

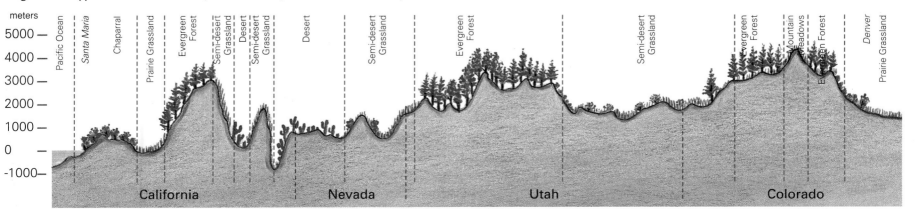

meters: 5000, 4000, 3000, 2000, 1000, 0, -1000

Cross section labels: Pacific Ocean, Santa Maria, Chaparral, Prairie Grassland, Evergreen Forest, Semi-desert Grassland, Desert, Semi-desert Grassland, Desert, Semi-desert Grassland, Evergreen Forest, Semi-desert Grassland, Evergreen Forest, Mountain Meadows, Evergreen Forest, Denver, Prairie Grassland

California   Nevada   Utah   Colorado

Advanced Civilizations

Latin America stretches from the northern border of Mexico to the tip of South America. It also includes some countries in the Caribbean. The "Latin" linking these nations is that they speak Spanish, Portuguese, or French — languages that are derived from the Latin language.

The area has a rich historical background. Highly advanced civilizations in the Americas were developed by Aztecs and Mayans in Mexico and northern Central America, and by Incas in Peru, Bolivia, and Ecuador. Engineering, architecture, art, weaving,

mathematics, astronomy, sculpture, metalwork, and music were possibly the most advanced in the world at the time. The Aztec and Mayan diets were based on the staple crop of corn, first cultivated in central Mexico. The Incas were dependent on the potato as a food supply. The arrival of the Spanish conquistadors in the 16th century brought these civilizations to an abrupt end. Today, of all the countries in Latin America, those bordering the Pacific Ocean have the highest number of Native Americans in their populations.

The Pacific Rim countries of Latin America are all located on the Rim of Fire. Volcanic eruptions, earthquakes, and land- or mudslides are common natural hazards along the mountainous belt running from northwestern Mexico to southern Chile. Productive farming regions are found where water and volcanic soils are combined — coffee as well as tropical and subtropical fruits and vegetables are major crops in the region. Many of these products are exported to markets in North America and Europe via the Panama Canal, the waterway linking the Atlantic and Pacific Oceans.

Tikal, in Guatemala, was an important center of Mayan culture and administration. The city was abandoned in approximately 1100 C.E. and was gradually overgrown by jungle. Archaeologists have been uncovering the ruins since Tikal was rediscovered in the mid 20th century.

Machu Picchu sits high in the Andes, approximately 80 km (50 mi.) from Cuzco, Peru. It is thought to have been the last stronghold of the Incas when the Spanish arrived in the 16th century. Like Tikal, it was abandoned and "lost" for many centuries until it was rediscovered in 1911. For this reason, Machu Picchu is often referred to as the "Lost City of the Incas".

Coffee is an important export for several Latin American nations. This photograph shows coffee beans growing on a mountainside in Colombia. The volcanic soils and abundant rainfall make these beans some of the best in the world.

Construction of the Panama Canal, linking the Pacific and Atlantic Oceans across the Isthmus of Panama, was begun in 1904 and continued for ten years before the canal opened. The canal is 82 km (51 mi.) long, has six locks, and crosses two natural lakes.

Population Density of Selected Countries

Country	Population Density People/km²	Population Density People/sq. mi.
Bolivia	7.5	19.5
Peru	17.8	46.1
Chile	18.5	47.9
Colombia	31.2	80.8
Panama	32.8	84.9
Nicaragua	32.9	85.2
Ecuador	37.2	96.3
Mexico	46.9	121.5
Honduras	47.4	122.8
Costa Rica	63.6	164.7
Guatemala	94.8	245.5
El Salvador	248.9	644.7

Ethnic Groups in Latin America

- Mestizo – 55%
- Amerindian – 23%
- European origin – 13%
- Other – 5%
- African origin/mulatto – 4%

Altitudinal Variations in Climate

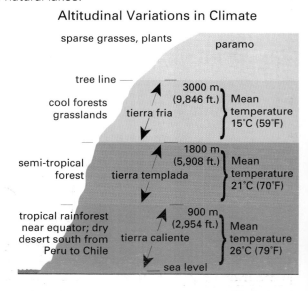

sparse grasses, plants — paramo

tree line

cool forests grasslands — tierra fria — 3000 m (9,846 ft.) — Mean temperature 15°C (59°F)

semi-tropical forest — tierra templada — 1800 m (5,908 ft.) — Mean temperature 21°C (70°F)

tropical rainforest near equator; dry desert south from Peru to Chile — tierra caliente — 900 m (2,954 ft.) — Mean temperature 26°C (79°F)

sea level

QUICK FACTS La Paz, Bolivia, at more than 3658 m (12,000 ft.), is the highest capital city in the world. Present-day Mexico City stands on the site of Tenochtitlán, the ancient Aztec capital. The capital of Spain's New World Empire was Lima, now capital of Peru.

The South Pacific Islands

The 25 000 islands in Oceania are divided into three main groups — Melanesia, Micronesia, and Polynesia. They are separated by great distances from each other and from much of the rest of the world.

There are some large islands, such as New Guinea. Others are quite small and appear as tiny dots on the map, if they appear at all.

Some island nations are in fact archipelagos, or chains of many small, separate islands.

Most of the islands of Oceania are of volcanic origin. Tahiti and Samoa, for example, are high islands, with tall volcanic mountains and fertile soils. Over time, the volcanic mountains are worn down or sink slowly into the ocean floor. As they do this,

coral reefs grow upward to form low, circular islands, such as the Marshall Islands. Eventually, the volcanic peak completely disappears below sea level, leaving behind an atoll — a coral reef that encloses a lagoon. Tarawa Atoll is a good example of this.

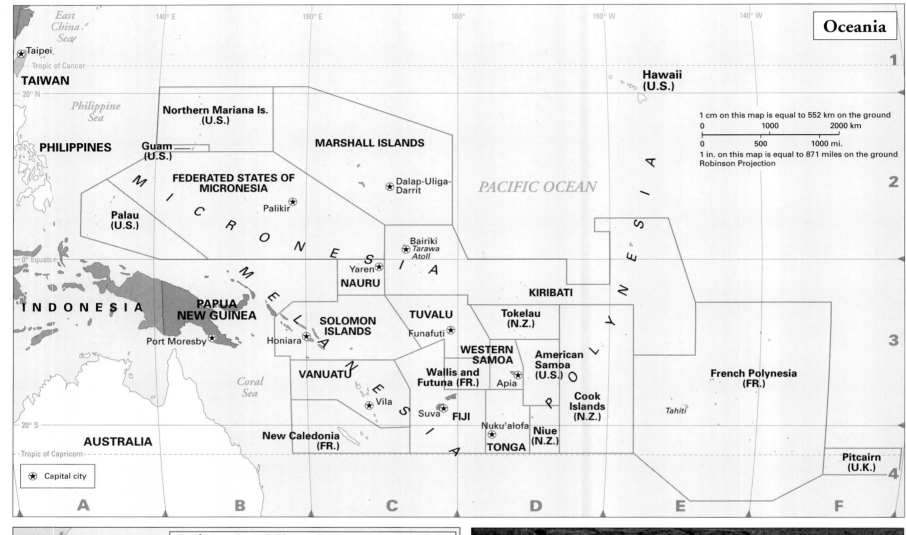

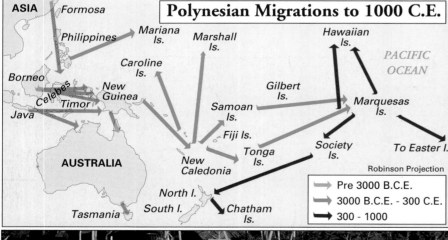

The Polynesian people developed "outrigger" canoes with long, thin floats on one or both side(s) to prevent them from capsizing. Using these and their methods of navigation, they traveled thousands of kilometers over open seas to colonize the islands of the Pacific.

Copra, one of Oceania's major exports, is the dried kernels of coconuts. The coconut oil that is extracted from copra is used to make cooking oil, margarine, soap, and cosmetics. Coconuts and tropical fruits, such as pineapples, grow well in the fertile volcanic soils of many Pacific islands.

QUICK FACTS   The Pacific Ocean contains 25% of the world's coral reefs.
Corals are animals, and reefs and islands are formed as millions of their skeletons build up.
There are more islands in the Pacific than in all the other oceans together.

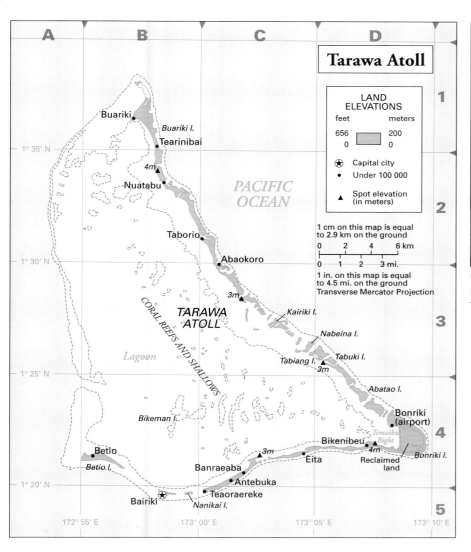

Tarawa Atoll

LAND ELEVATIONS

feet	meters
656	200
0	0

✪ Capital city
● Under 100 000
▲ Spot elevation (in meters)

1 cm on this map is equal to 2.9 km on the ground

0   2   4   6 km
0   1   2   3 mi.

1 in. on this map is equal to 4.5 mi. on the ground
Transverse Mercator Projection

PACIFIC OCEAN

Buariki
Buariki I.
Tearinibai
4m
Nuatabu
Taborio
Abaokoro
3m
TARAWA ATOLL
Kairiki I.
Nabeina I.
Tabuki I.
Tabiang I.
3m
CORAL REEFS AND SHALLOWS
Lagoon
Abatao I.
Bikeman I.
Bonriki (airport)
Temaiku Bight
Bikenibeu
Betio
4m
Banraeaba
3m
Eita
Reclaimed land
Bonriki I.
Betio I.
Antebuka
Teaoraereke
Bairiki
Nanikai I.

Coral reefs are mainly found in tropical waters where the temperature is more than 22°C (72°F) all year round. They are home to many varieties of fish and other marine life.

Types of Reef

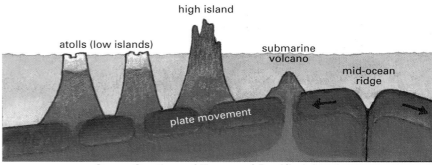

When the sea level is fairly constant, fringing reefs develop.

When the sea level rises or the land sinks, the coral grows upwards and a barrier reef is formed.

An atoll is a volcanic island that once had a fringing reef. As it sank, the coral reef grew upwards enclosing a lagoon.

high island

atolls (low islands)

submarine volcano

mid-ocean ridge

plate movement

Cross Section of Types of Pacific Islands

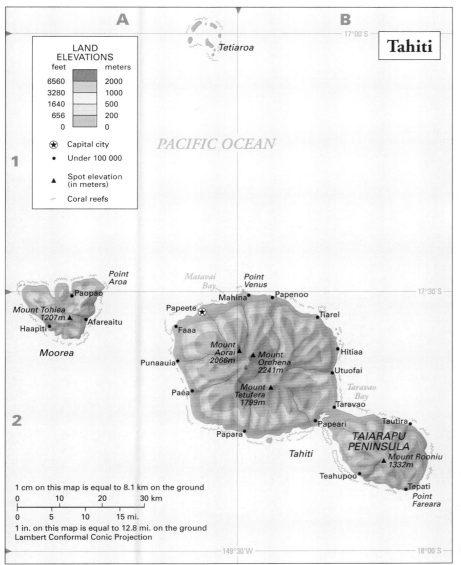

LAND ELEVATIONS

feet	meters
6560	2000
3280	1000
1640	500
656	200
0	0

✪ Capital city
● Under 100 000
▲ Spot elevation (in meters)
Coral reefs

Tahiti

Tetiaroa

PACIFIC OCEAN

Point Aroa
Paopao
Matavai Bay
Point Venus
Papenoo
Mahina
Papeete
Tiarel
Mount Tohiea 1207m
Afareaitu
Faaa
Haapiti
Hitiaa
Moorea
Mount Aorai 2066m
Mount Orohena 2241m
Punaauia
Utuofai
Mount Tetufera 1799m
Taravao Bay
Paéa
Taravao
Tautira
Papeari
Papara
TAIARAPU PENINSULA
Tahiti
Mount Rooniu 1332m
Teahupoo
Tepati
Point Fareara

1 cm on this map is equal to 8.1 km on the ground

0   10   20   30 km
0   5   10   15 mi.

1 in. on this map is equal to 12.8 mi. on the ground
Lambert Conformal Conic Projection

White sand beaches, warm tropical weather, and a turquoise ocean attract tourists in large numbers. In fact, tourism is the most important industry of many of the islands of Oceania.

"Land of the Long White Cloud"

The first Polynesians to arrive in New Zealand, more than 800 years ago, named it Aotearoa, or "Land of the Long White Cloud". This was how New Zealand looked to them when they saw it on the horizon after they had sailed hundreds of kilometers across open seas. Today, the population is a mixture of Polynesian and European peoples. The Polynesians are known as the Maori, while the Europeans are mainly of British descent.

New Zealand's position on the Pacific Rim of Fire means that it is a mountainous country, with only a small percentage of level land scattered along the coasts of both the North and South Islands. There are many volcanic features, including tall, graceful volcanic peaks, hot springs, and geysers in the North Island. In the South Island, the high Southern Alps, including Mount Cook, are covered with glaciers and icefields. The southwest coast is known as Fiordland because of the many fiords created as the sea flooded valleys gouged out by glaciers during the last Ice Age.

Sheep and dairy cattle thrive on New Zealand's pastures, kept constantly green by a mild, moist climate. The economy is heavily dependent on agriculture. If world demand or prices for agricultural products fall, the country's economy suffers. About 65% of New Zealand's exports are agricultural products, while it must import manufactured goods, energy, and minerals.

Like Australia, New Zealand is home to plants, birds, and animals that are found no place else on earth. One such animal, a reptile called the tuatara, is thought to be the last survivor of a species that became extinct over 100 million years ago.

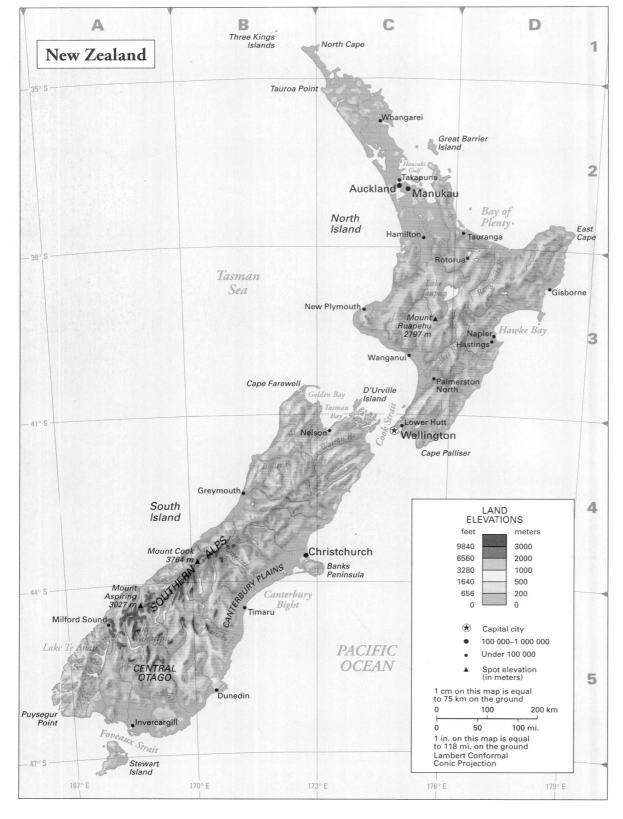

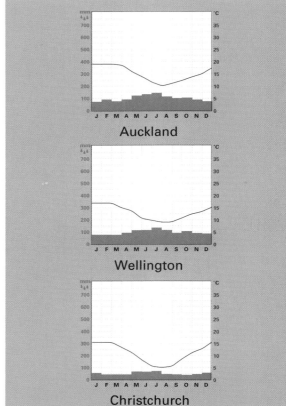

Auckland

Wellington

Christchurch

Wool is an important export in New Zealand. Sheep and wool account for approximately 30% of the country's agricultural production.

QUICK FACTS
Languages: English and Maori
Area: 270 990 km² (104,602 sq. mi.)

Population (1994): 3 498 000
Imports (1992): US$9 200 million
Exports (1992): US$9 338 million

87

Long ago, glaciers cut huge U-shaped valleys into the southwestern coast of New Zealand's South Island. Many of these glacial valleys have been flooded to form fiords, like this at Milford Sound. These are included in Fiordland National Park, a famous New Zealand site often seen on travel posters and in tourist guides.

Maori people retain much of their cultural identity, although they do not always dress in their traditional clothing. Those shown here are a concert party.

Trading Partners

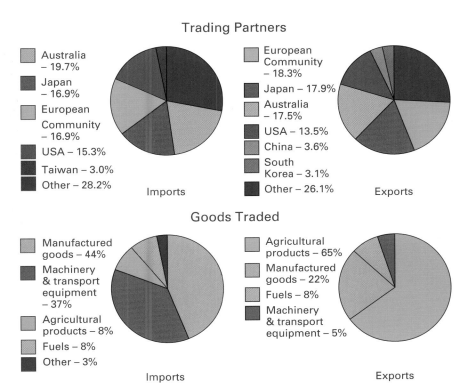

Australia – 19.7%
Japan – 16.9%
European Community – 16.9%
USA – 15.3%
Taiwan – 3.0%
Other – 28.2%

Imports

European Community – 18.3%
Japan – 17.9%
Australia – 17.5%
USA – 13.5%
China – 3.6%
South Korea – 3.1%
Other – 26.1%

Exports

Goods Traded

Manufactured goods – 44%
Machinery & transport equipment – 37%
Agricultural products – 8%
Fuels – 8%
Other – 3%

Imports

Agricultural products – 65%
Manufactured goods – 22%
Fuels – 8%
Machinery & transport equipment – 5%

Exports

Rotorua is at the center of an area where hot springs, boiling mud pools, and geysers are often seen. Geothermal energy is a renewable resource that is becoming increasingly important in many Pacific Rim countries, including Japan, New Zealand, and the United States.

Some species of albatross can have a wingspan of as much as 3.5 m (11.5 ft.). The bird's large, tapered wings make it an expert at gliding and flying.

The tuatara is found today on only a few islands off New Zealand's coast. Sometimes called a "living fossil", the tuatara is shaped like a miniature dinosaur, having a spiny ridge down its back, and a thick tail. It also has a vestigial, or undeveloped, third eye.

The kiwi is a flightless bird, native to New Zealand. It is about the same size as a large chicken. It has short legs and coarse, dark feathers hiding undeveloped wings that are of no use for flying.

Note: Animals are not drawn to scale.

The Island Continent

When North Americans are enjoying the summer heat, it is winter in Australia — the land in the southern hemisphere, or "down under". Australia is almost centered on the Tropic of Capricorn and is surrounded by large areas of water; thus, its climate is generally tropical to subtropical. Only in the highlands of the Great Dividing Range are colder temperatures and snow common during the winter months.

Australia is the only country that is also a continent. It is a large country and a country of contrasts. Much of the interior of Australia is a huge, largely unpopulated desert. Grasslands fringe this desert. Tropical rainforests are in the north, which is affected by monsoons. Australia also has low-lying coastal plains, averaging about 65 km (40 mi.) across. The eastern, southeastern, and southwestern coastal plains are the most densely populated areas of the land, and more than 85% of Australia's population are city dwellers.

Cut off from much of the rest of the world by large water bodies, Australia is home to many plants and animals that are found nowhere else on earth. The platypus, koala bear, kangaroo, wombat, and emu are just a few of such animals.

Australia is rich in natural resources, including bauxite, coal, iron ore, copper, tin, silver, uranium, nickel, tungsten, mineral sands, lead, zinc, diamonds, natural gas, and petroleum. The country exports large quantities of many of these. It is also a major exporter of wheat, meat, and dairy products, and usually produces more than 25% of the world's annual output of wool.

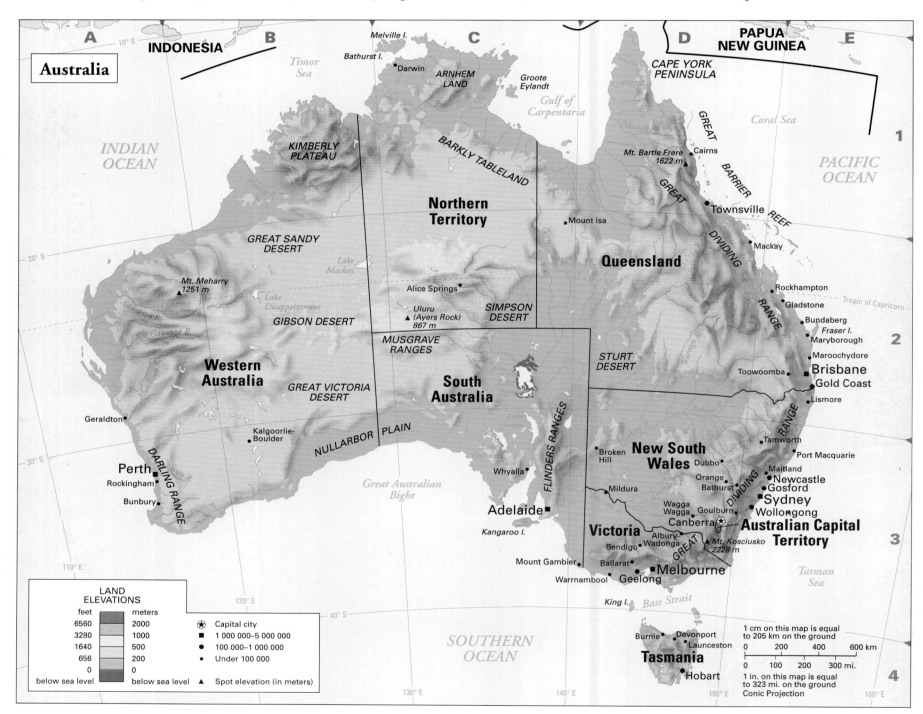

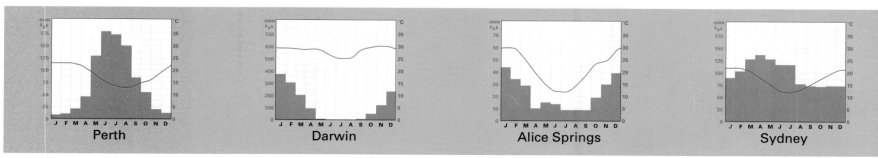

Perth   Darwin   Alice Springs   Sydney

QUICK FACTS
Language: English
Area: 7 686 850 km² (2,967,124 sq. mi.)

Population (1994): 7 843 000
Imports (1992): US$43 831 million
Exports (1992): US$42 439 million

89

Kakadu National Park

This aerial view looking east over Jim Jim Falls was taken during the wet season.

A coral reef is a complex, complete ecosystem in itself. Australia's Great Barrier Reef is the largest coral reef on earth. Like Kakadu National Park, the Great Barrier Reef is a World Heritage Site.

Kakadu National Park is home to many species of wildlife, including the wallaby seen here. There are crocodiles, water buffalo, kangaroos, and wild horses, called brumbies, in the park.

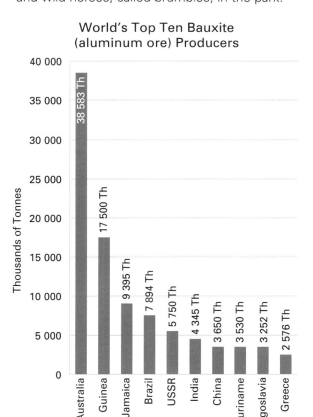

Cave paintings in Kakadu National Park vividly illustrate the culture and life of the Aborigines. Some of the animals shown in the paintings are now extinct.

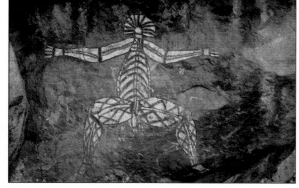

Agricultural goods such as wool, meat, and wheat are important to the Australian economy. Huge cattle ranches and sheep stations are located in the "outback", the grasslands surrounding the interior desert.

Sydney, Australia's largest city and main port, is famous all over the world for its distinctive Opera House, which is pictured on the right here. The city was founded in 1788 as a British colony.

World's Top Ten Bauxite (aluminum ore) Producers

Thousands of Tonnes

Country	Production (Th)
Australia	38 583 Th
Guinea	17 500 Th
Jamaica	9 395 Th
Brazil	7 894 Th
USSR	5 750 Th
India	4 345 Th
China	3 650 Th
Suriname	3 530 Th
Yugoslavia	3 252 Th
Greece	2 576 Th

Land Use

- Permanent Pasture – 58%
- Other – 22%
- Forest – 14%
- Arable Land – 6%

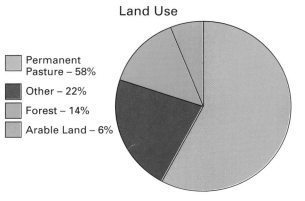

Pacific Connections

The nations of the Pacific Rim are linked by immigration, trade, tourism, and investment.

Many North Americans originally came from other Pacific Rim countries such as China, Hong Kong, Korea, Japan, Australia, New Zealand, and Mexico. Each immigrant has brought a part of his or her culture that has helped change and improve the face of many North American cities.

Stores all around the Pacific display a wonderful assortment of goods from the nations of the region. Apples from British Columbia are sold in Hong Kong, wheat from Canada and the United States travels to China and Russia, and Japanese cars are sold in many countries.

Millions of tourists cross the Pacific in both directions every year. Asian visitors ski the Rockies or visit National Parks in the Americas, while North American tourists enjoy Tahiti, Thailand, Australia, and New Zealand.

Sometimes, though, the links between Pacific partners are not so obvious. Japanese cars bought in North America could have been built in a plant in Ontario or Ohio. A forestry company in British Columbia might in fact be owned by another company in New Zealand.

▶ Walking tours in the Himalayas are popular with North American tourists. The mountains of Kashmir are beautiful and challenging.

Chinatown in San Francisco reflects that city's multicultural heritage and strong ties to other Pacific Rim countries.

A taxi in Hong Kong advertises apples from British Columbia. Trade in food items is an important link among Pacific Rim nations.

The Dash-8 aircraft, like the one shown here in Thailand, is designed and built in Canada.

QUICK FACTS
In 1992, 6 986 183 tourists visited Hong Kong.
In 1990, Americans spent US$38.7 billion as they toured abroad.

This worker at a vineyard in Chile is transferring wine to oak storage barrels prior to export.

Japanese and Korean pearls are sold around the world.

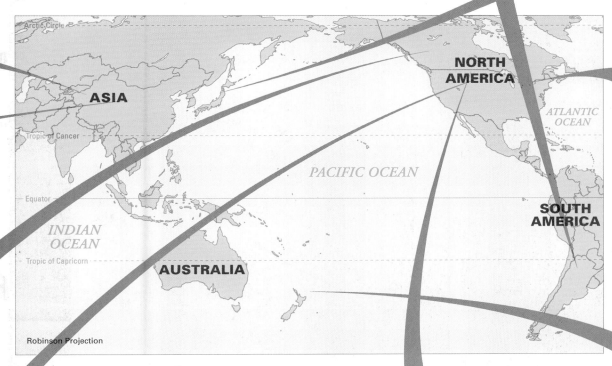

Baseball is a popular sport in Japan and other areas of Asia where American influence is strong.

North Americans find familiar sights as far away as Bangkok.

Bungee jumping, which originated in New Zealand, has become a popular sport in California and other parts of North America.

This gazetteer is a list of the place names on the physical and political maps. Beside each place name, in **bold type**, is the page number followed by the grid square(s). When a feature crosses over a political boundary or is on more than one map, the listing shows the location where the feature is shown best in its entirety.

Kansas City, USA **78-79** 2, D
Kanto Plain **70** 2-3, C-D
Kanto Range **70** 3, C
Kaohsiung, Taiwan **58** 4, B
Kashi, China **58** 3, A
Kashmir, India **44** 1, B
Kasumi, Lake **70** 2-3, D
Kathmandu, Nepal **12-13** 3, B
Kau Sai I. **57** 2, C
Kauai, Hawaiian Is. **16** 1, B
Kaula, Hawaiian Is. **16** 1, A
Kawaguchi, Japan **70** 3, C
Kawasaki, Japan **70** 3, C
Kazakhstan **72** 2, A-B
Kazan', Russia **72** 2, B
Kediri, Indonesia **53** 2, E
Kelowna, Canada **76** 4, E
Kendari, Indonesia **52** 2, F
Kenora, Canada **74-75** 5, C
Kentucky **78-79** 2, E
Kenya **8-9** 5-6, D-E
Kepulauan Kangean **53** 2, F
Kerinci, Mt. **52** 2, B
Ketapang, Indonesia **52** 2, C-D
Khabarovsk, Russia **72** 3, F
Kii Peninsula **70** 3-4, A-B
Kii Range **70** 3, A-B
Kimberly Plateau **88** 1, B
Kimch'aek, N. Korea **64** 2, C
Kimhae, S. Korea **64** 5, B
King George, Mt. **76** 3, E
King Island **88** 4, D
Kingston, Canada **74-75** 5, E
Kirgizstan **72** 2, B
Kiribati **84** 2-3, C-E
Kishiwada, Japan **70** 3, A
Kiso R. **70** 3, B
Kiso Range **70** 3, B
Kitakami R. **66** 3, D
Kitakyushu, Japan **66** 4, B
Kitchener, Canada **74-75** 5, D
Kitimat, Canada **76** 3, C
Klyuchevskaya Sopka **72** 2, F
Knoxville, USA **78-79** 2, E
Kobe, Japan **70** 3, A
Kochi, Japan **66** 4, B
Koje I. **64** 5, B
Koko Nur **58** 3, D
Kolyma Mountains **72** 1-2, F
Kolyma R. **72** 1-2, E-F
Komatsu, Japan **70** 2, B
Komsomolsk, Russia **72** 3, F
Kongur, Mt. **58** 3, A
Korea **64**
Korea Strait **64** 5-6, B-C
Koriyama, Japan **70** 2, D
Koryak Mts. **72** 1, F
Kosciusko, Mt. **88** 3, D
Kota Kinabalu, Malaysia **48-49** 3, C
Kowloon, Hong Kong **57** 3, C
Krakatoa, Indonesia **53** 2, A
Krasnoyarsk, Russia **72** 3, D
Krishna R. **44** 3, B-C
Kuala Lumpur, Malaysia **48-49** 3, B
Kuching, Malaysia **48-49** 3, C
Kudus, Indonesia **53** 2, D
Kum R. **64** 4-5, B
Kumagaya, Japan **70** 2, C
Kumai, Indonesia **52** 2, D
Kumamoto, Japan **66** 4, B
Kunlun Mts. **58** 3, B-C
Kunming, China **58** 4, D
Kunsan, S. Korea **64** 5, B
Kupang, Indonesia **52** 4, F
Kuril Islands **72** 2-3, F
Kushiro, Japan **66** 2, D
Kusong, N. Korea **64** 3, A
Kutch, Gulf of **44** 2, A-B
Kuwait **72** 3, A
Kwangju, S. Korea **64** 5, B
Kwanmo, Mt. **64** 2, C
Kwun Tong, Hong Kong **57** 3, C
Kyongju, S. Korea **64** 5, C
Kyoto **70** 3, A
Kyoto, Japan **70** 3, A
Kyushu **66** 4, A-B

L

La Paz, Bolivia **83** 5, D
Labrador City, Canada **74-75** 4, E
Labrador Sea **74-75** 3, E-F
Lachlan R. **88** 3, D
Lagunade Bay **54** 4-5, C-D
Lahat, Indonesia **52** 2, B
Lake of the Woods **74-75** 5, C
Lakshadweep **44** 3, B
Lamma I. **57** 3, B
Lamon Bay **54** 4, C

Lan I. **58** 4, C
Lanai, Hawaiian Is. **16** 1, B
Lansing, USA **78-79** 1, E
Lantau I. **57** 3, A-B
Lantau Pk. **57** 3, A
Lanzhou, China **58** 3, D
Laoag, Philippines **54** 2, C
Laos **48-49** 1-2, B
Lapland **6-7** 2, D
Laptev Sea **72** 1, C
Las Vegas, USA **78-79** 2, B
Latin America **83**
Latvia **8-9** 3, D
Launceston, Australia **88** 4, D
Lebanon **72** 2, A
Legazpi, Philippines **54** 5, D
Leon, Mexico **83** 11, I
Lesotho **8-9** 7, D
Lesser Antilles **83** 2, D
Lesser Sunda Islands **52** 3-4, D-G
Lethbridge, Canada **74-75** 4, B
Leyte Gulf **54** 6, E
Leyte, Philippines **54** 6, E
Lhasa, China **58** 4, C
Liao R. **58** 2, E-F
Liard R. **76** 2, C-D
Liberia **8-9** 5, B
Libya **8-9** 4, C-D
Libyan Desert **6-7** 4, D
Liechtenstein **8-9** 3, C (# 5)
Lima, Peru **83** 5, C
Lincoln, USA **78-79** 1, D
Lismore, Australia **88** 3, E
Lithuania **8-9** 3, D (#8)
Little Rock, USA **78-79** 2, D
Llanos **83** 3, C-D
Lloyd George, Mt. **76** 2, D
Loess Plateau **58** 3, D
Logan, Mt. **17** 1, B
London, Canada **74-75** 5, D
Long Beach, USA **78-79** 2, B
Longs Peak **17** 3, F
Los Angeles, USA **78-79** 2, B
Louisiana **78-79** 2-3, D-E
Louisville, USA **78-79** 2, E
Lower Guinea **6-7** 6, C
Lower Hutt, New Zealand **86** 4, C
Lu I. **57** 4, C
Lucena, Philippines **54** 5, C
Lucknow, India **44** 2, C
Ludhiana, India **44** 1, B
Luwuk, Indonesia **52** 2, F
Luxembourg **8-9** 3, C (# 3)
Luzon **54** 2-5, B-E
Luzon Strait **54** 1-2, C

M

Macau **12-13** 3, B
Macedonia, Former Yugoslav Republic of **8-9** 3, D (# 18)
Maceió, Brazil **83** 4, G
Mackay, Australia **88** 2, E
Mackay, Lake **88** 2, B
Mackenzie Mts. **17** 1, C-D
Mackenzie R. **17** 1, C-D
Macquarie R. **88** 3, D
Madagascar **8-9** 6-7, E
Madeira R. **83** 4, D
Madison, USA **78-79** 1, E
Madiun, Indonesia **53** 2, D
Madras, India **44** 3, C
Madura **53** 2, E
Madurai, India **44** 4, B
Maebashi, Japan **70** 2, C
Magadan, Russia **72** 2, F
Magdalena R. **83** 3, C
Magelang, Indonesia **53** 2, D
Magellan, Strait of **83** 9, C-D
Mahanadi R. **44** 2, C
Mahina, Tahiti **85** 2, B
Maine **78-79** 1, F-G
Maitland, Australia **88** 3, E
Maizuru **70** 3, A
Makassar Strait **52** 1-2, E
Malacca, Strait of **52** 1, A-B
Malang, Indonesia **53** 2, E
Malawi **8-9** 6, D
Malawi, L. **6-7** 6, D
Malay Pen. **48-49** 2-3, A-B
Malaysia **48-49** 3, B-C
Maldives **12-13** 4, A
Male, Maldives **12-13** 4, A
Mali **8-9** 4-5, B-C
Malta **8-9** 4, C (# 21)
Manado, Indonesia **52** 1, F
Managua, Nicaragua **83** 2, B

Manaus, Brazil **83** 4, D
Manchester, USA **78-79** 1, F
Manchurian Plain **58** 2, F
Mandalay, Myanmar **48-49** 1, A
Mandaue, Philippines **54** 6, D
Manila Bay **54** 4, C
Manila, Philippines **54** 4, C
Manitoba **74-75** 3-5, C
Manitoba, Lake **74-75** 4, C
Manokwari, Indonesia **52** 2, H
Manukau, New Zealand **86** 2, C
Maoke Mountains **52** 2, I
Mar del Plata, Argentina **83** 7, E
Maracaibo, L. **83** 2-3, C
Maracaibo, Venezuela **83** 2, C
Marañón R. **83** 4, C
Marapi, Mt. **52** 2, B
Marawi, Philippines **54** 7, E
Marinduque, Philippines **54** 5, C-D
Maroochydore, Australia **88** 2, E
Marshall Islands **84** 1-2, B-C
Maryborough, Australia **88** 2, E
Maryland **78-79** 2, F
Masan, S. Korea **64** 5, B
Masbate **54** 5-6, D
Massachusetts **78-79** 1, F (#3)
Mataram, Indonesia **52** 3, E
Matavai Bay **85** 2, A
Mato Grosso Plateau **83** 5, E
Matsue, Japan **66** 3, B
Matsumoto, Japan **70** 2, B
Matsuru, Japan **70** 3, A
Matsuyama, Japan **66** 4, B
Maui, Hawaiian Is. **16** 1, B
Mauna Kea **16** 2, B
Mauna Loa **16** 2, B
Mauritania **8-9** 4-5, B
Mauritius **8-9** 7, E
Medan, Indonesia **52** 1, A
Medellín, Colombia **83** 3, C
Medicine Hat, Canada **74-75** 4, B
Mediterranean Sea **6-7** 3-4, C-D
Meerut, India **44** 2, B
Meharry, Mt. **88** 2, A
Mekong R. **6-7** 4-5, H
Melanesia **84** 3-4, B-C
Melbourne, Australia **88** 3, D
Melville I. **88** 1, C
Memphis, USA **78-79** 2, E
Mentawai Islands **52** 2, A-B
Mentok, Indonesia **52** 2, C
Meratus Mts. **52** 2, E
Merauke, Indonesia **52** 3, I
Mérida, Mexico **83** 11, K
Mexico **83** 10-12, H-K
Mexico City, Mexico **83** 12, J
Mexico, Gulf of **6-7** 4-5, P
Miami, USA **78-79** 3, E
Michigan **78-79** 1, E
Michigan, Lake **78-79** 1, E
Micronesia **84** 2-3, A-C
Mie **70** 3-4, A-B
Milford Sound, New Zealand **86** 5, A
Milwaukee, USA **78-79** 1, E
Minahasa Peninsula **52** 1, F
Mindanao **54** 7-9, C-F
Mindanao R. **54** 8, C
Mindoro Strait **54** 5, C
Mindoro, Philippines **54** 5, C
Minneapolis, USA **78-79** 1, D
Minnesota **78-79** 1, D
Miri, Malaysia **48-49** 3, C
Misool Island **52** 2, G-H
Mississippi **78-79** 2, D-E
Mississippi R. **6-7** 3-4, P
Missouri **78-79** 1-2, D-E
Missouri R. **6-7** 3-4, O-P
Mitchell R. **88** 1, D
Mito, Japan **70** 2, D
Miyagi **70** 1-2, D
Miyazaki, Japan **66** 4, B
Mobile, USA **78-79** 2, E
Mogami R. **66** 3, C-D
Mokp'o, S. Korea **64** 5, B
Moldava **8-9** 3, D
Molokai, Hawaiian Is. **16** 1, B
Molucca Sea **52** 1-2, F-G
Moluccas **52** 1-2, G
Moncton, Canada **74-75** 4, F
Mongolia **72** 2, C
Mongolian Plateau **6-7** 3, H
Montana **78-79** 1, B-C
Monterrey, Mexico **83** 11, I
Montevideo, Uruguay **83** 7, E
Montgomery, USA **78-79** 2, E
Montpelier, USA **78-79** 1, F

Montréal, Canada **74-75** 5, E
Moorea **85** 1-2, A
Moose Jaw, Canada **74-75** 4, B
Morioka, Japan **66** 3, D
Moro Gulf **54** 8, D
Morocco **8-9** 4, B
Morotai **52** 1, G
Moscow, Russia **72** 2, B
Moulmein, Myanmar **48-49** 2, A
Mount Gambier, Australia **88** 3, D
Mozambique **8-9** 6-7, D
Muller Mts. **52** 1-2, D
Murchison R. **88** 2, A
Murmansk, Russia **72** 1, C
Murray R. **88** 3, C-D
Musgrave Ranges **88** 2, B-C
Muztag, Mt. **58** 3, B
Myanmar (Burma) **48-49** 1-2, A-B
Mysore Plateau **44** 3, B
Mysore, India **44** 3, B

N

Nabeina I. **85** 3, C
Nachi-Katsuura, Japan **70** 4, A
Naga Hills **44** 2, D
Naga, Philippines **54** 5, D
Nagano **70** 2-3, B-C
Nagano, Japan **70** 2, C
Nagaoka, Japan **70** 2, C
Nagasaki, Japan **66** 4, A
Nagoya, Japan **70** 3, B
Nagpur, India **44** 2, B
Naka R. **70** 2, C-D
Nakhodka, Russia **72** 3, F
Nakhon Ratchasima, Thailand **48-49** 2, B
Nakhon Si Thammarat, Thailand **48-49** 3, A
Naktong R. **64** 4-5, B
Nam Dinh, Vietnam **48-49** 1, B
Namibia **8-9** 6-7, C
Namoi R. **88** 3, D-E
Namp'o, N. Korea **64** 3, A
Nanaimo, Canada **76** 4, D
Nanchang, China **58** 4, E
Nanda Devi Peak **44** 1, B
Nangapinoh, Indonesia **52** 2, D
Nanikai I. **85** 3, C
Nanjing, China **58** 3, E
Nanning, China **58** 4, D
Napier, New Zealand **86** 3, D
Nara **70** 3-4, A-B
Nara, Japan **70** 3, A
Narmada R. **44** 2, B-C
Narodnaya, Mount **72** 2, C
Nashville, USA **78-79** 2, E
Nasik, India **44** 2, B
Natal, Brazil **83** 4, G
Nauru **84** 3, C
Nebraska **78-79** 1, C-D
Necker I., Hawaiian Is. **16** 1, A
Negro R., Argentina **83** 7-8, C-D
Negro R., Brazil **83** 4, D
Negros **54** 6-7, D
Nelson, Canada **74-75** 5, B
Nelson, New Zealand **86** 4, C
Nepal **72** 3, B
Netherlands **8-9** 3, C (# 1)
Nevada **78-79** 1-2, B
New Brunswick **74-75** 4, E-F
New Caledonia **84** 3-4, B-C
New Delhi, India **44** 2, B
New Guinea **48-49** 4, E-F
New Hampshire **78-79** 1, F (#2)
New Jersey **78-79** 1-2, F
New Kowloon, Hong Kong **57** 2, C
New Mexico **78-79** 2, C
New Orleans, USA **78-79** 3, D
New Plymouth, New Zealand **86** 3, C
New Siberian Islands **72** 1, E
New South Wales **88** 2-3, D-E
New Territories **57** 1-2, A-D
New York **78-79** 1, F
New York, USA **78-79** 1, F
New Zealand **86-87**
Newark, USA **78-79** 1, F
Newcastle, Australia **88** 3, E
Newfoundland **74-75** 3-4, E-F
Newfoundland **74-75** 3-4, F
Nha Trang, Vietnam **48-49** 2, B
Nias Island **52** 1, A
Nicaragua **83** 2, B
Nicobar Is. **44** 4, D
Niger **8-9** 4-5, C
Niger R. **6-7** 5, B-C
Nigeria **8-9** 5, C
Nihoa, Hawaiian Is. **16** 1, A
Niigata **70** 1-2, B-C
Niigata, Japan **70** 2, C

Stuart L. **76** 3, D
Sturt Desert **88** 2, D
Sucre, Bolivia **83** 5, D
Sudan **6-7** 5, B-C
Sudan **8-9** 4-5, D
Sudbury, Canada **74-75** 5, D
Sukabumi, Indonesia **53** 2, B
Sula Islands **52** 2, F-G
Sulawesi **48-49** 3-4, C-D
Sultan Alonto, Lake **54** 8, E
Sulu Archipelago **54** 8-9, B-C
Sulu Sea **54** 6-8, B-C
Sumatra **52** 1-3, A-C
Sumba **52** 3-4, E-F
Sumbawa **52** 3, E
Sunch'on, N. Korea **64** 3, A
Sunch'on, S. Korea **64** 5, B
Superior, Lake **78-79** 1, D-E
Surabaya, Indonesia **53** 2, E
Surakarta, Indonesia **53** 2, D
Surat, India **44** 2, B
Surigao, Philippines **54** 7, E
Suriname **83** 3, B
Suruga Bay **70** 3, C
Suva, Fiji **84** 3, C
Suwa, Lake **70** 2, C
Suwon, S. Korea **64** 4, B
Suzuka, Japan **70** 3, B
Svalbard **6-7** 2, C-D
Swan R. **88** 3, A
Swaziland **8-9** 7, D
Sweden **8-9** 2-3, C-D
Swift Current, Canada **74-75** 4, B
Switzerland **8-9** 3, C (# 4)
Sydney, Australia **88** 3, E
Sydney, Canada **74-75** 4, F
Syria **72** 2, A

T
Taan R. **58** 2, B-C
Tabiang I. **85** 3, C-D
Taborio, Tarawa Atoll **85** 2, C
Tabuki I. **85** 3, D
Tacloban, Philippines **54** 6, E
Tadzhikistan **72** 3, B
Taebaek Mts. **64** 4, B-C
Taedong R. **64** 3, B
Taegu, S. Korea **64** 5, B
Taejon, S. Korea **64** 4, B
Tahiti **85** 2, A-B
Tai Mo Pk. **57** 2, B
Taiarapu Peninsula **85** 2, B
Taichung, Taiwan **58** 2, B
Taimyr Pen. **6-7** 2, G-H
Tainan, Taiwan **58** 4, B
Taipei, Taiwan **58** 1, C
Taitung, Taiwan **58** 4, C
Taiwan **58**
Taiwan Strait **58** 2, A-B
Taiyuan, China **58** 3, E
Takamatsu, Japan **66** 4, B
Takaoka, Japan **70** 2, B
Takapuna, New Zealand **86** 2, C
Takasaki, Japan **70** 2, C
Taklimakan Desert **58** 3, A-B
Talaud Islands **52** 1, G
Tallahassee, USA **78-79** 2, E
Tampa, USA **78-79** 3, E
Tampines, Singapore **55** 2, C
Tamworth, Australia **88** 3, E
Tanahgrogot, Indonesia **52** 2, E
Tanahmerah, Indonesia **52** 3, I
Tanch'on, N. Korea **64** 2, B
Tanganyika, L. **6-7** 6, D
Tanimbar Islands **52** 3, H
Tanjungbatu, Indonesia **52** 1, E
Tanjungselor, Indonesia **52** 1, E
Tanzania **8-9** 6, D
Tap Mun I. **57** 2, D
Tapajós R. **83** 4, E
Tapan, Indonesia **52** 2, B
Tapti R. **44** 2, B
Tarakan, Indonesia **52** 1, E
Tarlac, Philippines **54** 4, C
Tasikmalaya, Indonesia **53** 2, C

Tasman Bay **86** 3-4, C
Tasman Sea **6-7** 7-8, J-K
Tasmania **88** 4, D
Tata Mailau, Mt. **52** 3, G
Taunggyi, Myanmar **48-49** 1, A
Taupo, Lake **86** 3, C-D
Tauranga, New Zealand **86** 2, D
Tauroa Point **86** 2, C
Tautira, Tahiti **85** 2, B
Tawitawi Group **54** 9, B-C
Tayshet, Russia **72** 3, D
Te Anau, Lake **86** 5, A
Teahupoo, Tahiti **85** 2, B
Teaoraereke, Tarawa Atoll **85** 5, C
Tearinibai, Tarawa Atoll **85** 1, B
Tegal, Indonesia **53** 2, C
Tegucigalpa, Honduras **83** 2, B
Tehuantepec, Isthmus of **83** 12, J
Tekong I. **55** 1-2, D
Telukbetung, Indonesia **52** 3, C
Temaiku Bight **85** 4, D
Tennessee **78-79** 2, E
Tenryu R. **70** 3, B
Tepati, Tahiti **85** 2, B
Ternate, Indonesia **52** 1, G
Terrace, Canada **76** 3, C
Teslin R. **76** 1-2, B
Tetiaroa **85** 1, A
Tetufera, Mount **85** 2, B
Texas **78-79** 2-3, C-D
Thailand **48-49** 1-3, A-B
Thana, India **44** 3, B
Thimphu, Bhutan **12-13** 3, B
Thompson R. **76** 3, D-E
Thompson, Canada **74-75** 4, C
Three Kings Islands **86** 1, B
Thunder Bay, Canada **74-75** 5, D
Tian Mts. **58** 2, B
Tianjin, China **58** 3, E
Tiarei, Tahiti **85** 2, B
Tibet, Plateau of **58** 3, B-C
Tien Shan **6-7** 3, F-G
Tierra del Fuego **83** 9, D
Tijuana, Mexico **83** 10, H
Tiksi, Russia **72** 1-2, E
Timah Hill **55** 2, B
Timaru, New Zealand **86** 5, B
Timmins, Canada **74-75** 5, D
Timor **52** 3-4, F-G
Timor Sea **52** 4, G
Titicaca, L. **83** 5, D
Tocantins R. **83** 4-5, F
Tochigi **70** 2, C-D
Togo **8-9** 5, C
Tohiea, Mount **85** 2, A
Tokch'on, N. Korea **64** 3, B
Tokelau **84** 3, D
Tokyo **70** 3, C
Tokyo Bay **70** 3, C
Tokyo, Japan **70** 3, C
Toledo, USA **78-79** 1, E
Tomakomai, Japan **66** 2, D
Tone R. **66** 2-3, C-D
Tonga **84** 3-4, D
Toowoomba, Australia **88** 2, E
Topeka, USA **78-79** 2, D
Toronto, Canada **74-75** 5, E
Torrens, L. **88** 2-3, D
Tottori, Japan **66** 3, B
Townsville, Australia **88** 1, D
Toyama **70** 2, B
Toyama, Japan **70** 2, B
Toyohashi, Japan **70** 3, B
Toyota, Japan **70** 3, B
Trail, Canada **74-75** 5, B
Trenton, USA **78-79** 1, F
Trinidad & Tobago **8-9** 5, Q
Tristan da Cunha **8-9** 7, B
Trivandrum, India **44** 4, B
Trujillo, Peru **83** 4, C
Tsing I. **57** 2, B
Tsu, Japan **70** 3, B
Tsuchiura, Japan **70** 2, D
Tsuen Wan, Hong Kong **57** 2, B
Tsugaru Strait **66** 2, D
Tsuruga, Japan **70** 3, B

Tucson, USA **78-79** 2, B
Tuen Mun, Hong Kong **57** 2, A
Tumen R. **64** 1-2, C
Tung Lung I. **57** 3, C
Tunisia **8-9** 4, C
Tura, Russia **72** 2, D
Turkey, **72** 2, A
Turkmenistan **72** 2-3, A-B
Turpan Depression **58** 2, B
Tuvalu **84** 3, C-D

U
Ubin I. **55** 1-2, C
Ufa, Russia **72** 2, B
Uganda **8-9** 5-6, D
Uichiura Bay **66** 2, D
Uijongbu, S. Korea **64** 4, B
Ujungpandang, Indonesia **52** 2, E
Ukraine **8-9** 3, D
Ulan Bator, Mongolia **12-13** 2, B
Ulan-Ude, Russia **72** 3, D
Ullung I. **64** 4, C
Ulsan, S. Korea **64** 5, C
Uluru (Ayers Rock) **88** 2, C
United Arab Emirates **72** 3, A
United Kingdom **8-9** 3, C
United States of America **78-79**
Upper Guinea **6-7** 5, B-C
Ural Mts. **72** 2, B-C
Ural R. **72** 2, B
Uruguay **83** 7, E
Uruguay R. **83** 6-7, E-F
Ürümqi, China **58** 2, B
Utah **78-79** 1-2, B-C
Utsomhomiya, Japan **70** 2, C
Utuofai, Tahiti **85** 2, C
Uzbekistan **72** 2-3, B

V
Vadodara, India **44** 2, B
Valdez, USA **78-79** 3, C
Valencia, Venezuela **83** 2, D
Valparaíso, Chile **83** 7, C
Vancouver Island **76** 3-4, C-D
Vancouver, Canada **76** 4, D
Vanderhoof, Canada **76** 3, D
Vanino, Russia **72** 3, F
Vanuatu **84** 3, C
Varanasi, India **44** 2, C
Venezuela **83** 2-3, C-D
Verkhoyansk Mts. **72** 2, E
Verkhoyansk, Russia **72** 2, E
Vermont **78-79** 1, F (#1)
Vernon, Canada **76** 3, E
Victoria (Xianggang), Hong Kong **57** 3, B
Victoria **88** 3, D
Victoria Island **74-75** 2, B-C
Victoria Pk. **57** 3, B
Victoria, Canada **76** 4, D
Victoria, L. **6-7** 6, D
Vietnam **48-49** 1-3, B
Vigan, Philippines **54** 3, C
Vijayawada, India **44** 3, C
Vila, Vanuatu **84** 3, C
Vindhya Range **44** 2, B
Vinh, Vietnam **48-49** 2, B
Virginia **78-79** 2, E-F
Visayan Islands **54** 5-6, C-E
Visayan Sea **54** 6, D-E
Vishakhapatnam, India **44** 3, C
Vladivostok, Russia **72** 3, F
Volga R. **72** 2, B-C
Volgograd, Russia **72** 2, B
Voronezh, Russia **72** 2, B
Vrangelya **72** 1, F

W
Waddington, Mt. **76** 3, C
Wagga Wagga, Australia **88** 3, D
Waigeo Island **52** 2, H
Waikaro R. **86** 2-3, C-D
Wairau R. **86** 4, B-C
Waitaki R. **86** 5, B
Wajima, Japan **70** 2, B
Wakatipu, Lake **86** 5, A
Wakayama **70** 3-4, A
Wakayama, Japan **70** 3, A
Wallis and Futuna **84** 3, C-D

Wanganui, New Zealand **86** 3, C
Warrego R. **88** 2, D
Warrnambool, Australia **88** 3, D
Washington **78-79** 1, A-B
Washington, D. C., USA **78-79** 2, F
Wellington, New Zealand **86** 4, C
West Korea Bay **64** 3, A
West Siberian Plain **72** 2, C-D
West Virginia **78-79** 2, E-F (#4)
Western Australia **88** 1-3, A-B
Western Ghats **44** 3, B
Western Sahara **8-9** 4, B
Western Samoa **84** 3, D
Wetar Island **52** 3, G
Whangarei, New Zealand **86** 2, C
Wheeling, USA **78-79** 1, E
Whitehorse, Canada **74-75** 3, A
Whitney, Mt. **17** 4, E
Whyalla, Australia **88** 3, C
Wichita, USA **78-79** 2, D
Williams Lake, Canada **76** 3, D
Williston L. **76** 2, C
Windsor, Canada **74-75** 5, D
Winnipeg, Canada **74-75** 5, C
Winnipeg, Lake **74-75** 4, C
Winnipegosis, Lake **74-75** 4, C
Wisconsin **78-79** 1, D-E
Wollongong, Australia **88** 3, E
Wonju, S. Korea **64** 4, B
Wonsan, N. Korea **64** 3, B
Woodlands, Singapore **55** 1, B
World: Physical **6-7**
World: Polar Projections **11**
World: Political **8-9**
World: Time Zones **10**
Wuhan, China **58** 3, E
Wyoming **78-79** 1, B-C

X
Xi R. **58** 4, E
Xi'an, China **58** 3, D
Xianggang I. **57** 3, C
Xingu R. **83** 4-5, E
Xining, China **58** 3, D

Y
Yakutsk, Russia **72** 2, E
Yalu R. **64** 2, A-B
Yamagata **70** 1-2, C-D
Yamagata, Japan **70** 1, D
Yamanashi **70** 3, C
Yamuna R. **44** 1-2, B-C
Yangon (Rangoon), Myanmar **48-49** 2, A
Yapen Island **52** 2, I
Yaren, Nauru **84** 3, C
Yari-ga, Mt. **70** 2, B
Yekaterinburg, Russia **72** 2, C
Yellow Sea **58** 2-3, E-F
Yellowknife, Canada **74-75** 3, B
Yemen **72** 3, A
Yenisey R. **72** 1-3, D
Yinchuan, China **58** 3, D
Yishun, Singapore **55** 1, C
Yodo R. **70** 3, A
Yogyakarta, Indonesia **53** 2, D
Yokkaichi, Japan **70** 3, B
Yokohama, Japan **70** 3, C
Yosu, S. Korea **64** 5, B
You R. **58** 4, D
Yu Shan **58** 3, B-C
Yucatán Pen. **83** 11-12, K
Yuen Long, Hong Kong **57** 2, A
Yugoslavia **8-9** 3, D (# 16)
Yukon R. **17** 1, A-C
Yukon Territory **74-75** 2-3, A-B
Yumen, China **58** 3, C

Z
Zagros Mts. **6-7** 4, E
Zaire **8-9** 5-6, C-D
Zambezi R. **6-7** 6, D
Zambia **8-9** 6, D
Zamboanga Peninsula **54** 7-8, C-D
Zamboanga, Philippines **54** 8, D
Zhengzhou, China **58** 3, E
Zimbabwe **8-9** 6-7, D